How to Pass

NATIONAL 5

Art & Design

Elaine Boylan and Stephanie Lightbown

HODDER GIBSON
AN HACHETTE UK COMPANY

Orders: please contact Bookpoint Ltd, 130 Park Drive, Abingdon, Oxon OX14 4SE. Telephone: (44) 01235 827720. Fax: (44) 01235 400454. Lines are open 9.00–5.00, Monday to Saturday, with a 24-hour message answering service. Visit our website at www.hoddereducation.co.uk. Hodder Gibson can be contacted direct on: Tel: 0141 848 1609; Fax: 0141 889 6315; email: hoddergibson@hodder.co.uk

© Elaine Boylan, Stephanie Lightbown 2013
First published in 2013 by
Hodder Gibson, an imprint of Hodder Education,
An Hachette UK Company,
2a Christie Street
Paisley PA1 1NB

Impression number   5 4 3 2
Year   2017 2016 2015 2014

Cover photo © Nicolle Phillips
Illustrations by Aptara, Inc.
Typeset in Cronos Pro by Aptara, Inc.
Printed in Spain
A catalogue record for this title is available from the British Library
ISBN: 978 1 4441 8732 8

Contents

Introduction

This book is designed to help you to complete your Art & Design coursework successfully and to help you prepare for the written examination. It should help you to understand the course structure and how marks are allocated. A unique aspect of this book is the guidance which is included on the practical aspects of the course, which account for 80% of the marks.

Advice to users

The book contains overviews of the key aspects of the National 5 Art & Design course:

> Expressive Activity with integrated Critical Studies

> Design Activity with integrated Critical Studies

> Question Paper

These sections will outline the process you should follow in order to fulfil the assessment standards. Expressive and design techniques are also included to help you when you are developing your own practical work.

Case studies

In each section, case studies are shown to give you further insights into the course and to give ideas of different approaches. These have been developed from real students' work. The work used is of a particularly high standard so that you can see what good quality work at this level might look like.

In Art & Design, there are no right or wrong answers – it is not like Maths! It is important that you understand that there are many different ways of achieving the assessment standards. The case studies should help you to develop your own ways.

We have deliberately selected case studies in popular areas of expressive Art & Design. Although it is impossible to cover every type of Portfolio within the scope of this book, whichever area you are working in, you will be able to gain inspiration and ideas which you can apply to your own work.

External assessment – the Portfolio gallery

A unique feature of this book is that it contains a visual representation of what Portfolios look like when they are hung up for external marking. This should let you see how different formats work and to see how important it is that your own Portfolio has visual impact and coherence.

Feature boxes

HINTS & TIPS

Examiner's tips are included throughout the book. This advice should help you to maximise your **marks**.

COMMON MISTAKES

Throughout the book, alerts will be given on **problems** which cause candidates to lose marks.

Teacher's feedback

Throughout the case studies, there are teacher's notes to let you see the feedback given at various stages. This should help you to understand the process followed by the candidate.

National 4

Throughout the book, guidance is given for National 4 candidates, where there is a difference in requirements. Although, there are some differences, N4 students can follow much the same process as those doing the N5 course. N4 candidates who follow the guidelines given in this book for the Expressive and Design practical Activities with integrated Critical Studies should overtake the Assessment Standards for National 4 (as long as the work is of the required quality).

The main differences for National 4 candidates are:

- There is no written exam
- Work is internally assessed so a Portfolio does not have to be submitted
- Assessment is on a pass/fail basis
- Work will be levelled at SCQF level 4 rather than 5.

Chapter 1

Course Structure

COMPONENT	ASSESSMENT ARRANGEMENTS		MARKS AVAILABLE
Expressive Activity	Unit	Internal assessment	Pass/fail
	Portfolio	External assessment	80
Design Activity	Unit	Internal assessment	Pass/fail
	Portfolio	External assessment	80
Question Paper	Examination	External assessment	40
		TOTAL	200

Percentage of marks for each component

Expressive Portfolio **40%**

Design Portfolio **40%**

Question Paper **20%**

Final mark **100%**

National 4

As there is no examination at National 4 level, your assessment is based on the practical and critical work you have carried out in your Expressive, Design and Added Value Units. This work is assessed on a pass/fail basis. Although you only need to meet the minimum standard to pass, you should try to do your best possible work. This will be to your advantage if you progress to National 5 later, as your skills will be more developed.

HINTS & TIPS

You should be aware that your Unit work is separate from your Portfolio. Your Unit work will be retained by your teacher as SQA sometimes carry out checks to ensure it has been completed.

Skills and knowledge

In this course, you are being assessed on your ability to:

respond to a theme or brief in an effective and imaginative way

communicate personal thoughts, feelings and ideas

demonstrate problem solving, critical thinking and decision-making skills

plan, develop, produce and present creative art and design work

reflect on and evaluate art and design work

use art and design materials, techniques and technology in a creative and skillful way

understand how artists and designers use materials and techniques for creative and visual effect

understand the influence of social and cultural factors on art and design practice

Time management

Good time management is key to achieving success in the course. It doesn't matter how talented you are, if you don't get the work done in time, your grade will be badly affected. Your teacher has to submit your work for assessment, and will instruct you to have your work completed well ahead of the SQA deadline. This is to allow your work to be checked and labelled. There are also important departmental quality assurance and administration procedures to be carried out.

Schools deliver the course in different ways, but your school will probably use one of the following three models:

Your school may cover the Design Activity first followed by the Expressive Activity:

Design Activity with Critical Studies	Expressive Activity with Critical Studies	Course Assessment: Portfolio submission

You might do the Expressive Activity followed by the Design Activity:

Expressive Activity with Critical Studies	Design Activity with Critical Studies	Course Assessment: Portfolio submission

Some schools do both activities concurrently. This means that you will complete your Expressive and Design Activities at the same time, dividing your lessons each week between both:

Expressive Activity with Critical Studies	Course Assessment: Portfolio submission
Design Activity with Critical Studies	

It doesn't matter which way your school delivers the course, but you should ensure that you are aware of key deadlines and which tasks are expected to be completed. Use the table on the following page to record your main deadlines. If you have not been given this information, ask your teacher.

You will also find that the Expressive Activity and Design Activity checklists in this book will help you to keep track of your progress and make sure you have completed all of the tasks required.

Homework

Your teacher may give you specific homework tasks which will help you work towards completing your Units and Portfolio on time. If you are struggling to complete tasks in class time, consider doing some extra homework. Ask your teacher what you are allowed to take home to complete.

If you are not given homework, there are many tasks which you can do at home to save time in class and help you to produce a good quality Portfolio.

Homework tasks which you could do might include:

- market research for design
- research on related artists and designers
- initial sketch ideas for your Design and Expressive Units
- line drawings for your Expressive Portfolio which can be worked on in class.

Use your initiative! Refer to the case studies and advice on techniques in this book to develop your own work.

HINTS & TIPS

When you are setting aside time for a task, work out how much time you think you need, then double it – practical tasks always take longer than you think!

HINTS & TIPS

Make sure that you leave plenty of time for the final Expressive outcome and Design solution. It is important that you achieve the highest level of finish that you can. This should be the best work you have ever produced!

KEY DEADLINES			
	Task	Date	✓
Expressive Activity			
Unit	Initial studies, developments and experimental work completed		
	Integrated Critical Studies completed		
Portfolio	Selection of idea for further development		
	Development completed		
	Evaluation of development and decision on outcome		
	Final outcome completed		
	Evaluation completed		
	Presentation of Expressive Portfolio completed		
Design Activity			
Unit	Design brief completed		
	Research and initial development of ideas completed		
	Integrated Critical Studies completed		
Portfolio	Selection of idea for further development		
	Development completed		
	Evaluation of development and decision on design solution		
	Design solution completed		
	Evaluation completed		
	Presentation of Design Portfolio completed		
Critical Studies Question Paper			
Question Paper	Prelim exam		
	SQA exam		

Chapter 2

2 Expressive Activity

Introduction and overview

What is expressive art?

Expressive art is about communicating your own personal ideas in a visual way. There are a variety of expressive media, techniques and approaches to choose from and these should reflect the artist's personal preferences and style.

What will I be doing in this activity?

The creative process

In your Expressive Activity, you will be following a **creative process:**

Title/Theme/Stimulus

Investigation and research

Development

Final outcome

Evaluation

You will be producing a **Portfolio** of expressive artwork in response to a **title**, **theme** or **stimulus**.

Title
Theme
Stimulus

Possible approaches

Inspirational artists' work

National 4

You will follow the same creative process and you can use the same starting points suggested for National 5.

Be careful to choose an achievable topic as you are still developing your basic expressive skills at this level.

Responding to a theme or stimulus

Themes suggest a variety of things to different people and allow you to make a **personal** response.

It is a good idea to have a title as a starting point for your project, as this will help give it direction. Genres themselves are not titles. For instance, 'Still Life' or 'Portraiture' would not be suitable, as they are far too open-ended and don't suggest anything in particular.

You should choose a title, phrase or image, which suggests visual ideas, such as 'Living in a Fantasy World', 'On Closer Inspection', 'Reflections', 'Deep in Thought', 'Breakfast', 'Urban Decay', 'Childhood Memories', 'Collection', 'Afternoon Tea', 'Making Music', 'Me, Myself and I'. The possibilities are endless!

Alternatively, you could use a **stimulus**. This could be an object or a place. Maybe a line from a poem or song could provide inspiration. Your starting point could perhaps be an artist's work or a photograph which you like.

HINTS & TIPS

Your teacher may supply a choice of titles/themes/stimuli, or you may be asked to come up with your own idea. Make sure that you choose something you find genuinely interesting and which gives you lots of visual ideas.

Working within a genre

You might choose to work within one particular **genre** (category):

PORTRAITURE

or

FIGURE COMPOSITION

or

STILL LIFE

or

THE NATURAL ENVIRONMENT

or

THE BUILT ENVIRONMENT

Working across genres

You may also choose to work across genres, for instance producing:

- a portrait set in a built environment
- a still life set in the natural environment
- a figure composition in a landscape
- a fantasy scene incorporating aspects of several genres.

Another important aspect you will need to think about at the outset is the **approach** you will take. Your teacher will advise you about what is realistic. You may want to think about (or ask your teacher):

- Will this project be about 2D or 3D work or a mixture of both?
- Which **techniques** will I be using? (e.g. painting, drawing, print-making, mixed-media, sculpture, low relief)
- Do I need to provide the **subject matter** (e.g. objects, images, photographs), or will departmental resources be available?

NOTE: Your teacher may offer you a limited choice. This is because departments often specialise in one or two areas which they have the expertise, equipment and resources to deliver. This ensures that you get the support and resources that you need to complete the project.

Your teacher also has to consider your level of skill and make sure that you don't attempt something that will be too far beyond your ability and experience.

HINTS & TIPS

As well as researching and writing about artists, you could try to copy their style in a piece of work of your own. This is a great way to help you understand an artist's technique.

You will also complete some **Critical Studies** work. This should be related to the approach and subject matter you have selected. The Critical Studies tasks will help you to understand some key issues in expressive art and to develop your own approaches and techniques.

Your teacher will probably suggest some appropriate artists and artworks for you to investigate and analyse. Refer to the Case Studies to see how other candidates have approached this and to the section on the Question Paper.

Successful artists are:

Receptive to new experiences

Expressive art is like taking a journey without a map. You should be willing to explore, try new techniques, see what happens and where the journey takes you. Don't be too fixed in your thinking.

Observant

To produce successful artwork, it is necessary to have good observational skills. This will help you to notice the qualities of the different subjects you are looking at, and to learn how to use techniques effectively.

Focused

Expressive art requires a high level of concentration. Often, when you reach this level of focus, you will find that time seems to pass very quickly. Some people call this being 'in the zone'.

Committed and engaged

You will feel frustrated at times. Sometimes things won't work out. This is all part of the process of discovery, so try to see the positive side. Perhaps a technique isn't for you, or you don't have enough experience with it yet. Keep trying and don't give in!

Good at taking advice without taking it personally

If you feel as if you've put your heart and soul into something, only to be told of its faults, it can be difficult. Remember, your teacher is giving you constructive advice. Try to bear in mind, any criticism is about your work, not you, so take it positively and move on.

Self-critical

Push yourself to produce your best work. Students often think they are finished when there is more to be done. Try to notice missing details and whether tonal values are correct without having to ask your teacher.

Creative

Some expressive approaches seem to allow for more creativity than others but, whatever your choice of subject, it is important to demonstrate that you can work in an imaginative way, particularly in the development stage of the process. This could be something as simple as trying different viewpoints in a still life composition, or varying your media.

Willing to put the time in to improve and develop their own style

The only way to get better at drawing and a variety of expressive techniques is to practise. Unfortunately, there are no shortcuts! As well as noticing that your accuracy increases, you should find that your pace of work improves and that your confidence grows. The more you practise, the more likely it is that you will notice your own style developing.

Research and investigation

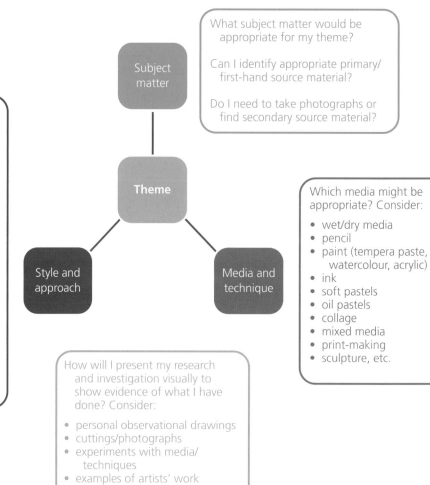

Which artists will inspire and influence my work?

What style will it be?

Which key visual elements interest me the most?

Consider:

- colour
- line
- tone
- shape
- form
- pattern
- texture

Will I work within one genre or work across genres?

What would be an appropriate scale for my work?

Subject matter

What subject matter would be appropriate for my theme?

Can I identify appropriate primary/first-hand source material?

Do I need to take photographs or find secondary source material?

Theme

Style and approach

Media and technique

Which media might be appropriate? Consider:

- wet/dry media
- pencil
- paint (tempera paste, watercolour, acrylic)
- ink
- soft pastels
- oil pastels
- collage
- mixed media
- print-making
- sculpture, etc.

How will I present my research and investigation visually to show evidence of what I have done? Consider:

- personal observational drawings
- cuttings/photographs
- experiments with media/techniques
- examples of artists' work
- annotations

Where will I find what I need?

Development

Initial ideas	• Consider a number of different possibilities in response to your theme • Produce a range of initial development studies
Selection of best idea	• Evaluate work done so far to see which idea is the best – remember to consider your theme • Select the best idea for further development
Development and refinement of selected idea	• Experiment with composition – think about viewpoint and arrangement • Explore media techniques

Evaluating expressive work

Evaluation is an important aspect of your work. It is also a task many people find difficult. This section will help you to understand the purpose of evaluation and will help you to build your skills in this area.

Evaluation involves making judgements and giving reasons. It can be about:

- what worked well
- what went wrong
- how successful or unsuccessful it is
- advantages and disadvantages of an approach
- whether everything went to plan, or why it didn't
- how well you managed your time
- the effectiveness of decisions you made
- how well an outcome reflects the theme
- whether you would approach a similar task in a different way in future
- skills that you developed.

What should I evaluate in my Expressive Activity?

The creative process

The final outcome

HINTS & TIPS

Try to vary your vocabulary so that your comments are not repetitive. You could use the wordbanks in this book or refer to a thesaurus. Developing your vocabulary will help you communicate your thoughts more clearly.

COMMON MISTAKES

Instead of evaluating, students sometimes describe their work, or tell the story of what they did. This is *not* evaluation.

How to develop descriptive comments into evaluative comments

BASIC AND DESCRIPTIVE COMMENT	EVALUATIVE COMMENT
My work is based on the title 'On Closer Inspection'. Tell us a bit more.	I chose the title 'On Closer Inspection' as it gave me lots of creative possibilities. I decided to interpret the title by developing some close-up still life ideas as I enjoy drawing objects and I like detail.
I used photography during the development stage. How did this help you?	I found using photography to develop compositions in my Unit helped me to frame the objects and try different arrangements. This was a quick method which helped me decide which compositions I wanted to develop further.
This picture is done using tempera paste. The marker can see this.	I found tempera paste difficult to control at first, but as you can see in this study, I am now more confident and able to show tonal values and detail effectively with this medium. I also like the vibrant colour and brushwork.
This is a drawing of a red pepper. We can see this!	For this study I decided to cut the red pepper in half as it gave some extra detail and made this line drawing more interesting.
I added a background to my portrait. Why, and for what effect?	I was inspired by the artist Joan Eardley to try a collage background technique. I developed the idea of a graffiti wall as a background and used some of her techniques to achieve this. I feel this gives an urban feel to the work and fits with my theme of 'Street Life'.
I used a 3D mixed media technique here. Expand on this.	I used some found objects in this work to explore a 3D mixed media technique as I was inspired by the work of Will Maclean in my Critical Studies.
I am happy with my expressive outcome. You need to give reasons.	My outcome worked out well. I like the way I incorporated the figure into a rundown urban background as this adds a 'story' to the picture and reflects my theme of 'Down and Out'. The downcast expression of the subject also helps convey a despondent mood.

How your Expressive Unit relates to your Portfolio

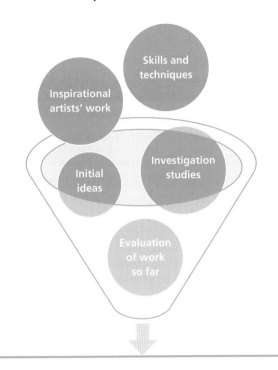

Expressive Unit work

- Skills and techniques
- Inspirational artists' work
- Initial ideas
- Investigation studies
- Evaluation of work so far

Unit

The Unit is marked on a pass or fail basis

Your Unit work will be retained in school for internal assessment

Portfolio

Selection of the **best idea** for further development

Compositional ideas and exploration of techniques

Reflection on effectiveness of developments

Completion of final expressive outcome

Evaluation of outcome in terms of how well it reflects the theme/title

Presentation of work for external assessment

Portfolio

36 marks available for this part of the Portfolio

36 marks for the outcome

8 marks for evaluation

Your finished Portfolio will be sent to SQA for external assessment

National 4

Your work does not need to be sent to SQA for external assessment so you do not need to present it as a Portfolio. Your teacher will advise you on what format your work should be for internal assessment.

Your final outcome is an important part of your Added Value Unit, which you need to complete to achieve your course award.

Use the checklist on this page to help you keep track of your Expressive Activity and to ensure that you meet the assessment standards. For submission to SQA, you may find that your teacher will help you with the presentation or labelling of your Portfolio, or you may be required to do this by yourself.

	Task	Success criteria	✓
EXPRESSIVE ACTIVITY CHECKLIST			
1	Starting point	I have selected a theme/title/stimulus.	
2	Research	I have completed a number of observational studies of subject matter related to my theme/title/stimulus.	
		I have Critical Studies work to prove that I have learned about a range of artists/art movements who work in my area of expressive art (including at least one contemporary artist).	
		From my Critical Studies, I have selected and analysed relevant works by at least two artists whose style/technique/subject matter relate to my own Expressive Activity.	
		I have included annotations to explain my thoughts and decisions.	
3	Development	I have completed a range of initial compositional developments which explore my theme/title/stimulus.	
		I have explored a variety of relevant materials and/or techniques.	
		I have selected the most successful idea for further development.	
		I have produced a range of further developments based on this one idea, exploring it through adapting and refining the composition, media and technique.	
		I have evaluated my work and added annotations to explain my thoughts and decisions.	
4	Final outcome	I have planned my final outcome, taking account of the time, resources, materials and skills required.	
		I have produced my outcome to the best standard I am capable of.	
		If appropriate (for 3D work), I have photographed my outcome, or arranged for it to be photographed.	
		I have evaluated my outcome, referring to the original theme/title/stimulus.	
5	Portfolio presentation	I have discussed the most suitable presentation format with my teacher, considering shape and size of card/paper.	
		I have selected the *relevant* work from my Expressive Activity which demonstrates my progress towards the final outcome.	
		I have arranged my work into a suitable layout, so that the creative process is clear, and checked this with my teacher before proceeding.	
		I have carefully and neatly stuck down my work, including my outcome, or photographs of my outcome.	
		Evaluation of my research and development work is included in the form of annotations.	
		I have included evaluation of my outcome in an appropriate format.	
		The separate sheets of my Portfolio have been securely taped together on the back.	
		The labels supplied by SQA have been stuck onto the back of my Portfolio.	
Well done – you've made it!			

'Flotsam & jetsam'

STILL LIFE CASE STUDY

2

- Investigation and research
- Creating compositions
- Using technology
- Critical Studies
- Development studies
- Artistic influences
- Outcome

Investigation and research

Emily's teacher had a selection of still life themes for her to choose from. The theme that appealed to her most was 'Flotsam & Jetsam'. At this stage, Emily began exploring observational drawing and media handling techniques. Emily drew a variety of objects relating to her theme. Emily's teacher encouraged her to work from primary source materials (drawing objects that are in front of you).

HINTS & TIPS

Good quality drawings and paintings are the key to this project. Choose objects that tell a story or fit into your theme. Pick different sizes of objects, use a variety of heights, shapes, forms, textures and colours.

Emily began exploring her preferred techniques: acrylic paint, watercolour and coloured pencil. Her confidence increased as she developed these techniques. She began to really enjoy painting and wanted to develop this further in her Portfolio.

Creating compositions

To develop compositional ideas in her Unit, Emily began by using a viewfinder and her camera. She positioned the objects into an interesting composition. By using her camera, she found it easier to experiment with unusual viewpoints.

Emily tried out a variety of compositions. She photographed the objects from above, which she did not like. She then cropped an image to create a square format. Emily liked the yellow lantern with the red reflector as her focal point.

HINTS & TIPS

To create compositional ideas, use a viewfinder or your camera's screen. Isolate the key elements in a scene and check their placement using the viewfinder. This makes it easier to compose your objects. Consider the number of objects in your composition. An odd number of elements will usually look better than an even number.

Emily varied her compositional studies and placed the objects with a strong horizontal emphasis. The bottle created a vertical focal point on the right-hand side of the image. Emily experimented further and created a more balanced composition by placing the bottle centrally.

Emily liked the vertical emphasis of the bottle and decided to explore this in one of her compositional studies.

Emily zoomed in to an area to create impact. Cropping objects helps to create tension but also focuses attention on certain areas of the composition. Emily considered how the objects were spaced, varying the space between the elements in her composition. Overlapping objects can create a busy and interesting composition.

Using technology

COMMON MISTAKES

Photography is a great way to develop compositional ideas. However, sometimes students are tempted to copy their photographs using tracing paper or a light box, or even to work over photocopies of the images with media. This is very obvious to markers. If you do this in your Expressive Portfolio, it will affect your mark as you are not demonstrating that you have met the assessment standards – you are required to show skill in observational drawing and media handling.

Emily began exploring one particular photograph by using digital imaging software. She found that she could quickly create changes. She decided to produce some thumbnails after this exercise to help with her expressive development.

The focal point

The focal point of a painting is what draws the viewer's eye to it. It is usually the main aspect you first notice when you look at the composition.

The Rule of Thirds

You can place your objects on the 'intersection points' from a Rule of Thirds grid. Check that the objects in the painting lead the eye towards the focal point.

Is there variety?

Try not to use the same type of composition all the time, no matter how successful it is. Vary where you put the horizon line, where you put the focal point, swap between portrait and landscape format compositions.

HINTS & TIPS

Remember to photograph your compositions from different viewpoints. Try zooming into a composition to create unusual development studies. It is important to create balance. Experiment with objects of different sizes and consider the effect of colour.

Critical studies

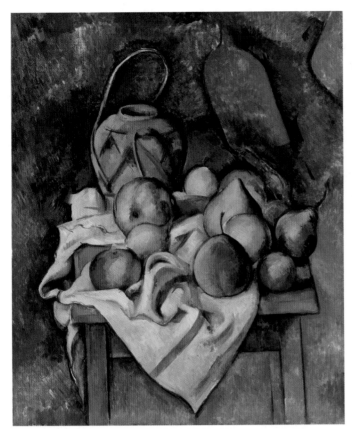

Le Vase Paille (1895) by Paul Cezanne

During her Unit, Emily studied a variety of still life artists in her Critical Studies. She took inspiration from Paul Cezanne because she found that his technique was particularly relevant to how she painted. She liked his use of visible brushwork and, after investigating his techniques, she concentrated on using expressive brushwork to emphasise the form of the objects. Emily found that Cezanne's subject matter was not particularly relevant to her own work but she liked his use of colour. Cezanne's muted colour palette with emphasis on applying and blending his colours with small brushstrokes inspired Emily.

Still Life with Seven Apples (1878) by Paul Cezanne

Shelves of Fruit (1995) by Leon Morrocco

Emily loved Leon Morrocco's work but knew that his strong vibrant colour palette did not suit her own work. She decided to experiment with his techniques of framing still life compositions with a seascape. She also liked how he would often compose objects on a shelf and use patterned fabric to provide a vertical emphasis.

Development studies for the Portfolio

After completing some quick development studies in her Unit sketchbook, Emily decided on the choice of objects for her Portfolio developments. She loved the ship's lantern and wanted this to be one of her main objects. She had some issues with all the other objects being smaller in comparison to the lantern. Her teacher advised her to include the wooden floats to allow for a more dynamic composition.

HINTS & TIPS

Develop thumbnails of your compositions. Thumbnails are small-scale sketches which quickly allow you to see a variety of viewpoints, create different focal points and see how objects relate to each other in terms of scale and colour.

Emily loved the result of this painted composition. The brushwork and depth of colour was strong. Cezanne's influence can be clearly seen. She took the advice of her teacher not to be scared of applying more colours through layers of paint. You can see Emily's confidence increasing in her compositional studies.

Artistic influences

In her sketchbook, Emily completed a number of small thumbnail studies exploring different seascapes which could be used as her background. She eventually decided to use a dark stormy seascape. Emily decided that the range of tonal blues would enhance the yellow of the ship's lantern. The warm and cold colour contrast will create a dynamic final composition.

Still Life looking towards Stromboli and Panarea by Leon Morrocco

'I am really interested in Morrocco's background seascape, which contrasts with the still life objects in the foreground. I think I will try to complete some development studies to see if this would work in my painting. Morrocco used warm and cold colours in many of his studies. The cold colours help the background to recede and the warm coloured objects appear to come closer to the viewer.'

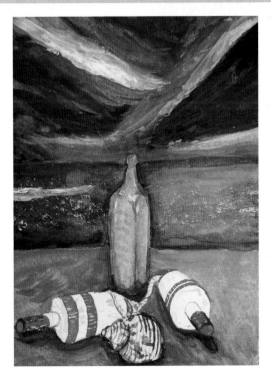

Outcome for the Portfolio

Emily's evaluation

'I experimented with a number of finishes and I felt that the acrylic paint technique that I had used in my smaller study of the glass bottle was definitely my most successful media handling technique. This gave me the confidence to embark on my larger composition.

I had decided that I would place a seascape in the background of my study and I spent a lot of time finding an appropriate image. I really liked the concrete wall which my objects sat on. I am really pleased with the effect of the seascape in my still life composition. The influence of Morrocco can be clearly seen here with the use of an interesting background which leads your eye to the foreground of my painting. I am particularly pleased with my brushwork which adds form to the objects and gives a strong atmospheric quality to my painting.'

'Dulce et decorum est'

2

- Investigation and research
- Critical Studies
- Development of narrative
- Composition and media handling
- Outcome

Investigation and research

Beth decided to work with a title and a narrative to develop her Expressive Activity. She loved history and was especially interested in World War I. She was keen to explore a more emotional response to this theme.

First, Beth explored several possible titles using key phrases to help her with her creative development. She found war quotes and phrases which inspired her initial Unit development:

- World War I
- Chemical warfare
- War games
- Peace versus war
- Conflict
- Gassing
- Bio hazard

She explored each of these titles in her Unit, mainly through spidergrams and thumbnail sketches. Her breakthrough came when she researched war literature and poetry. Discovering the poem *Dulce et Decorum Est* by Wilfred Owen became a pivotal moment in her Expressive Activity. She analysed the poem and picked out this particular verse:

Gas! Gas! Quick, boys! — An ecstasy of fumbling,
Fitting the clumsy helmets just in time;
But someone still was yelling out and stumbling,
And flound'ring like a man in fire or lime ...
Dim, through the misty panes and thick green light,
As under a green sea, I saw him drowning.

Beth's drawing of a gas mask using the medium of coloured pencils was very successful due to the strength of application. She also enjoyed painting the skull. This image was to become a key element in later development studies, with the skull being explored in a variety of media and techniques.

Critical studies

Pipe, Glass, Bottle of Vieux Marc (1914)
by Pablo Picasso
© 2012 Estate of Pablo Picasso/Artists
Rights Society (ARS), New York

Beth spent time in her Unit studying art that portrays war. She looked at war artists through posters, photography and painting.

Beth became increasingly interested in the technique of collage because she wanted to incorporate text with an image. She researched where collage had been used in expressive art and found that Picasso had used printed text in his paintings during his Cubist period. He used this technique to enhance the meaning of his still life works.

Weeping Woman (1937) by Pablo Picasso
© Pablo Picasso, 1937/Succession Pablo
Picasso, Paris

The Troubled City (1991) by Ken Currie

After further research she also found that Picasso had completed a series of paintings depicting the horrors of the Spanish Civil War. The painting *Weeping Woman* (1937) particularly inspired Beth. The emotion conveyed by a woman crying appealed to Beth but the green hues used by Picasso gave her the confidence to try her own version, which was more realistic but conveyed a symbolic message through the use of colour.

Head of an Idealist (1990) by Ken Currie
© All Rights 2012 Future Museum Project Partners

Ken Currie was the second artist Beth investigated. Beth found his war paintings difficult to look at because of the scenes of civil unrest that Currie depicted. In one painting, the figures were burning books and beating up men. It reminded Beth of television footage she had seen. She could relate to the subject matter that Currie had portrayed and liked the dark, sombre tones of his paintings.

Beth studied further work by Currie and found his later portraiture work really inspiring. *Head of an Idealist* was one of her favourites because of the skeletal face, which reminded her of her own skull study. Currie had also used text in the background, and Beth found the tattooed hands reinforced the message of the painting. This portrait had a luminous quality about it through Currie's dramatic use of light. The colour palette was limited, using muted dark, earthy tones which gave the portrait a sinister quality.

Development of theme

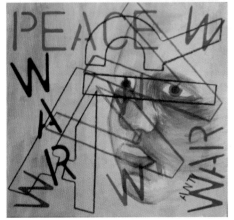

Beth decided her main focus would be the emotional aspect of war and particularly the gassing incident described in the poem. She used a pen and wash technique in her thumbnail portrait and then tried an emotional pose to convey the effects of war. Some of these studies remained in her sketchbook and were not developed further in her Portfolio.

Teacher's feedback

Beth, your observational drawings and paintings are excellent. I like the thumbnail compositions. The study of half your face combined with the skull demonstrates how difficult it is to achieve a realistic appearance. You seem to have lost the language and narrative evident in your earlier work. I would advise you to start incorporating text into your next developments.

At this point, Beth began to experiment with text-based art, in which she had previously expressed an interest in her Critical Studies.

Incorporating text into her work became one of Beth's main techniques. In her Critical Studies she had looked at collage and the Cubists. She began to use their technique of incorporating related language to help explain the painting. This was particularly successful in the gas mask composition.

Composition and media handling

Beth explored a variety of media techniques. She worked on prepared grounds, which included marbled paper, and used paint, pen and wash, collage, coloured pencil and oil pastel. She decided she wanted to use a mixed-media approach in her final outcome.

Beth developed many of her compositions by zooming in and cropping sketches that were originally larger to focus in on key areas. She used a viewfinder to help her with this approach.

She spent time exploring the skull, which symbolised death, and kept her main colour palette to a range of muted greens. The green colour palette symbolised the poem's lines, '*And flound'ring like a man in fire or lime... Dim, through the misty panes and thick green light*'. She found that by using the complementary colour of red, it enhanced the green tones and also represented the word *fire*.

Outcome for the Portfolio

'I feel that I have achieved certain aspects of my theme. I am pleased with my visual interpretation of the poem by Wilfred Owen, and the use of my colour palette of red and green which symbolised gas and fire. I love the background of newsprint, paint and stencilling. The result was better than I expected.

If I was completing this outcome again, I would like to improve the proportions of the face. I find my self-portrait difficult to evaluate because it is me, but I am pleased with the painting technique I developed in my portfolio.'

EXPRESSIVE MEDIA TECHNIQUES

2

- Tonal studies
- Paints
- Coloured pencils
- Tonal printmaking and charcoal
- Chalk and collage
- Drawing techniques
- Printmaking, batik and oil pastels
- Mixed media and 3D relief
- Ceramics

Tonal studies

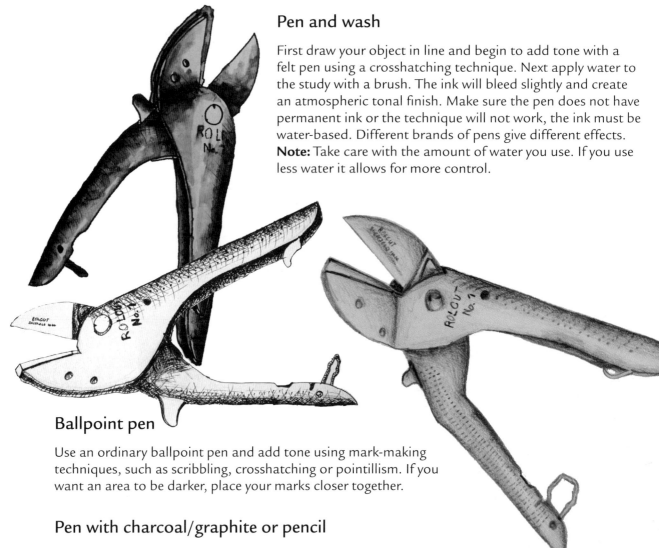

Pen and wash

First draw your object in line and begin to add tone with a felt pen using a crosshatching technique. Next apply water to the study with a brush. The ink will bleed slightly and create an atmospheric tonal finish. Make sure the pen does not have permanent ink or the technique will not work, the ink must be water-based. Different brands of pens give different effects. **Note:** Take care with the amount of water you use. If you use less water it allows for more control.

Ballpoint pen

Use an ordinary ballpoint pen and add tone using mark-making techniques, such as scribbling, crosshatching or pointillism. If you want an area to be darker, place your marks closer together.

Pen with charcoal/graphite or pencil

These are the most commonly used media for tonal studies. It is important for your drawing to have a range of tonal values – light, medium and dark.

Pen with watercolour wash

Begin your study using an ordinary ballpoint pen and then apply a wash of watercolour paint. This should be a light wash of paint (watery), not thick paint, or you will cover your drawing.

Coloured ballpoint pen

Try blue ballpoint pen worked over with watercolour for another variation using this technique.

Paints

Watercolour, gouache, acrylics, tempera paste and tempera blocks are all paints commonly used in schools. Each type of paint gives a different effect. It is only through experimentation that you can see which medium you prefer. Watercolour usually gives a subtle and delicate transparent finish. Gouache and tempera paste can be in tubes, tubs or in blocks and is similar to a water-based paint like watercolour, but can be applied more thickly and is often opaque. Acrylic paint can be applied either opaquely or with a transparent wash. It dries very quickly and is excellent for creating strong, expressive brush marks. Although acrylic is water-based, it becomes permanent when dry, so can be overworked without the colours underneath bleeding through.

There are a number of different painting techniques. You can work wet on wet to blend colours, or use dry brushwork (lightly brushing wet paint over dry paint) to create a dramatic effect. This technique is great for applying highlights and detail to your painting.

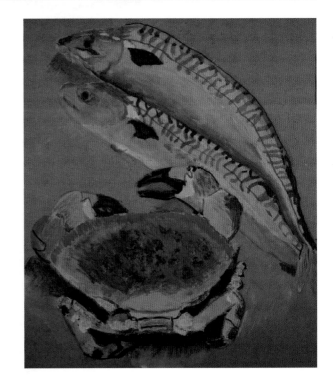

HINTS & TIPS

Using different qualities of paper with the same media can create very different outcomes. So if you like a certain medium, such as coloured pencil, try different papers, such as textured paper, brown or black paper, coloured or prepared papers.

Coloured pencils

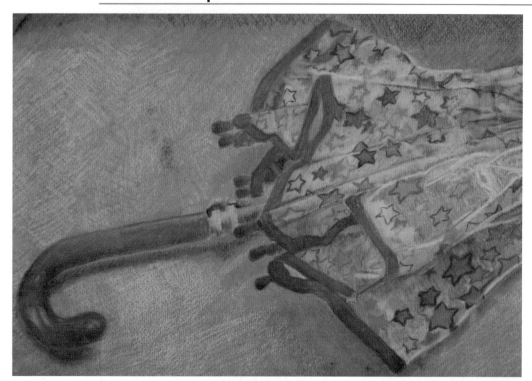

Coloured pencils are a good medium to use as they are quick and easy to learn to use well. They are also a versatile medium and can be used to enhance other media such as paint.

Shade the area carefully and build up the tones gradually. It is important to apply the colour slowly but strongly. Aim to capture contrasts of dark and light. The direction of your pencil marks will help to suggest form.

Artist-quality soft coloured pencils are good for blending colours together. You can overlay a variety of different colours to give a drawing depth. Different techniques you can use include cross hatching, shading and overlaying.

Tonal printmaking and charcoal

Polyprint

This is an unusual technique which can give quick results. Take a prepared polyprint block onto which you have already transferred a line drawing. Instead of rolling on the ink, paint onto the block with the printing ink instead. You need to use block printing ink, which will not dry out as you are working. Use black and white or shades and tints of one colour. For best results print on slightly damp, stretched paper. You will need to blot your print with scrap paper to remove any excess ink.

HINTS & TIPS

The brown paper background gives this white, grey and black coloured pencil study a different quality. A range of tonal values (dark, medium and light tones) have been used to make the objects appear 3D.

Charcoal

Charcoal is a medium which can be used to create strong tonal contrast. This drawing medium is expressive and can also be used with chalk pastel to highlight or add a hint of colour. Charcoal studies can be created by using your rubber as a drawing tool to rub in highlights.

Chalk and collage

Chalk pastels

Chalk pastels are soft colour pigments compressed into a stick. You can use chalk in a controlled mark-making technique on its own, or use pastels over paint to add emphasis or highlights. Chalk pastels can be easily blended and are very versatile, and can be used to create a subtle effect or for a more expressive mark-making technique. Pastels should be used on a coloured or black background to achieve the best results. They work best on slightly textured, rough paper.

Collage

Get some magazines and tear out some images that have the same colours and tones as your subject. Tear or cut these pictures into small pieces and glue them in a mosaic-like technique, matching the colours and tones to create your own image.

Drawing techniques

Continuous line drawing

Continuous line is a great method of producing drawings which have a lovely fresh quality. The technique is simple: take a pen and keep it in contact with the paper until you have completed the entire drawing. It is also a very good way of improving your observational skills.

Pointillism

Pointillism is a well-known technique which can be used with a variety of media. The technique is very simple to achieve. You can use a pen, oil pastel or paint brush to build up the dots. Darker tones are achieved by placing the dots closer together. You can also use a thicker pen to create the darker areas or block in very dark areas entirely.

Printmaking, batik and oil pastels

Printmaking

Printmaking is a versatile approach to produce a different type of development study or a final outcome. The main types of printmaking used in schools are monoprint, polyprint, lino cut and block print.

Paper batik

Paper batik is an unusual technique which can produce interesting results. Make a line drawing in pencil on white cartridge. Go over your pencil lines heavily with chalk. Use tempera paste which has been mixed to a thick and creamy consistency to paint inside the chalk lines. If you mix the colours with white paint to produce tints, it tends to give you more reliable results. Allow the painting to dry overnight and then test a separate small sample by painting over with waterproof ink. Some brands of ink are not effective and you will not want to ruin your work!

Place your finished inked painting on a drawing board in the sink and gently wash off with running water. A watering can is a good idea as it is gentle enough not to wash away your entire painting. Be patient with the washing-off stage. If there are any stubborn areas, rub very gently with a small sponge. You will gradually see your painting revealed.

Oil pastels

Oil pastel is a versatile and quick medium. You can use a dotted pointillism technique or small linear marks to create a range of tonal values. You can also create highlights and texture by using a cocktail stick to remove some of the oil pastel and reveal the colour underneath.

Mixed media and 3D low relief

Mixed media

Mixed media can be very effective in altering a painting or drawing that is not working. You have nothing to lose by adding another layer of media to an image that is not successful. By adding a textural technique over an existing painting, you can enhance the painting and give it depth or atmosphere.

Texture

Texture in painting can be created by adding materials such as sand, wood shavings or eggshells to PVA glue. This mixture can be added to the surface and painted over. This 3D effect creates texture.

Form can be suggested by building up areas of the work with layers of corrugated card. This technique works best if you apply a layer of tissue paper all over before you start painting to tidy and blend in the edges.

Gluing layers of tissue paper to the surface before you start painting can add another quality to your work. Gesso (a type of primer used by artists) can also be used to add textural effects before you start to paint.

Ceramics

Ceramics can be a great method of expressing yourself three dimensionally. Make sure your Art & Design department has a kiln and clay facilities before you decide to develop a ceramic project. Some schools specialise in this type of work and have teachers with a lot of knowledge in this area.

There are many finishes and glazes that you can use to achieve an interesting finish to your finished work. Iron oxide is a simple finish that helps to bring out the texture of the work, but you can also use acrylic paint. All-over colour effects tend to work best.

There are various methods that you can use to produce work in clay, from coils, slab work and low relief to other ceramic-media handling techniques. It requires a certain amount of specialist knowledge and planning. There are health and safety issues regarding the use of clay which your classroom teacher can advise on.

Chapter 3

3 Design Activity

Introduction and overview

What is design?

Design is about solving a problem, about planning how something will look and function, and how it will be made. It is about meeting the needs of a client or target market.

What will I be doing in this activity?

You will be producing a **Portfolio** of design work in response to a **design brief**.

You will work within a particular design area:

> **GRAPHICS**
> or
> **PRODUCT DESIGN**
> or
> **ARCHITECTURAL/ENVIRONMENTAL/INTERIOR DESIGN**
> or
> **JEWELLERY**
> or
> **FASHION/TEXTILES**

NOTE: Your teacher may not offer you a choice or may offer you a limited choice. This is because departments often specialise in one or two areas which they have the expertise, equipment and resources to deliver. This ensures that you get the support and resources you need to complete the project.

You will also complete some **Critical Studies** work. This should be related to the design area you have selected. The design studies tasks will help you to understand the key issues in your chosen design area.

The design process

In your Design Activity, you will be following a **design process**:

Your design brief

The design process is essentially a problem-solving activity, which you complete step by step. The first step is the design brief, which gives you information on requirements and constraints (restrictions). Your brief should be specific enough to give you the information you need but open-ended enough to allow you to be creative.

Your brief should contain information on:

HINTS & TIPS

It is worthwhile spending time getting your design brief right as it will make a difference to the success of the activity as a whole.

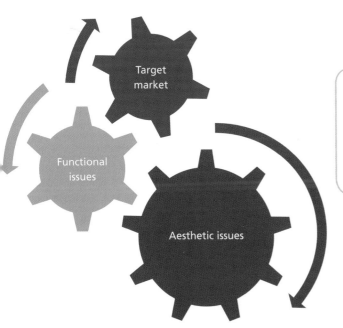

National 4

You will follow a similar design process to National 5 candidates. However, the development of the selected idea at N5 level requires to be explored in more depth.

Writing your brief

Your teacher may give you a design brief, and this is acceptable, but you may be asked to generate your own, or to adapt a basic brief.

Here are some examples to help you to understand what makes an effective design brief:

GRAPHIC DESIGN
Design a poster for a music festival.   Far too open-ended – there isn't enough information.
Design a poster. It should contain an image of a piano and Art Deco style lettering.   Too restrictive!
Design a poster for a music festival. The festival will feature jazz music and your design should communicate this through your choice of imagery, lettering, layout, colour and style. The festival will take place at Strathclyde Park on 14th July, starting at 2.30 pm.   Much better!

JEWELLERY DESIGN
Design a piece of jewellery based on nature.   Too open-ended – where would you begin?
Design a brooch which looks like a flower. It should appeal to teenage girls so the colour should be pink.   No scope for creativity.
You have been commissioned to design a piece of statement jewellery. The client is in her mid-20s and is a collector of unusual jewellery. Her style is theatrical and unorthodox and your jewellery design should demonstrate this. The piece should be a large-scale brooch, inspired by sea creatures. Your choice of materials and colour scheme should reflect the inspiration. The piece should be durable enough for special-occasion wear and you should consider suitable fastenings.   Scope to be creative and plenty of information. Well done!

HINTS & TIPS

Ensure that your design brief is realistic and achievable. For instance, it might be unrealistic to say that you will design a prom dress if you have no experience of sewing and garment construction, and have a limited budget.

Successful designers are:

Curious

You should explore all the aspects of your design brief. What are you being asked to do? What do you need to find out? Then go and investigate!

Open-minded

Don't be too fixed in your thinking. Be willing to change your mind depending on what you discover and how your ideas develop.

Creative and imaginative

In the early stages, when you are producing your Unit work, it is important to come up with several ideas. This is often difficult for young designers. You may find that you have a fixed idea about what your design solution will look like. Remember – you haven't been through the design process yet and you are unlikely to have come up with your best idea at the start.

Not afraid to take risks

It is a fact that you will learn more from what doesn't work than from your successes, so never be afraid to experiment and try things. This is particularly important in the first stages of the project.

Determined

At times, you will feel like you're 'stuck'. This is normal! If you work through this, you will be at your most creative. Try to approach the problem from different angles. Try a new technique. Try rearranging a design. Try making things bigger, smaller, whatever. It is important to keep going and you will suddenly find that you have come up with new, and probably better, solutions.

Good at taking advice

Think about your teacher as representing your 'client'. It's their job to make suggestions, to point out what's not working, to tell you if you're not fulfilling the original brief. Take this feedback positively. This is how real designers find out what they need to know to refine their ideas.

Good at meeting deadlines

Your work is submitted for external assessment, so you have to finish it on time! It is important to meet all of the interim deadlines set by your teacher, as well as the final deadline, otherwise you will run out of time and may not be able to finish your final outcome to the best standard, which will affect your mark.

Good at making judgements and decisions

It is really important that you choose your best initial idea to develop for the Portfolio as this will be the work that your mark is derived from.

HINTS & TIPS

Good time management is key to the success of this activity. If you miss one interim deadline, this may have a knock-on effect on the rest of your project. You may find that you have to rush to finish at the end.

Research and investigation

This is the part of the process where you should be thinking about what you need to find out to solve your design problem successfully. If you have produced an effective design brief, this will give you some clues about what you need to investigate.

At this point, it's worth spending some time planning what you are going to do. The following diagram should give you some ideas:

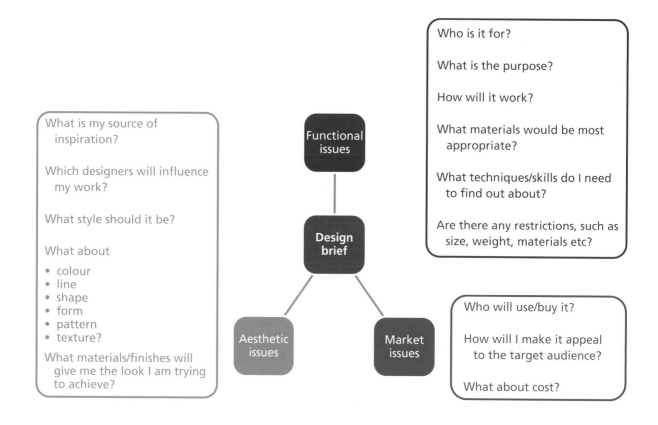

What is my source of inspiration?

Which designers will influence my work?

What style should it be?

What about
- colour
- line
- shape
- form
- pattern
- texture?

What materials/finishes will give me the look I am trying to achieve?

Functional issues

Who is it for?

What is the purpose?

How will it work?

What materials would be most appropriate?

What techniques/skills do I need to find out about?

Are there any restrictions, such as size, weight, materials etc?

Design brief

Aesthetic issues

Market issues

Who will use/buy it?

How will I make it appeal to the target audience?

What about cost?

How will I present my research and investigation visually to show evidence of what I have done? Consider:
- images – photos/cuttings/print-outs
- personal drawing
- samples of materials/techniques
- examples of designers' work
- market research
- information
- annotation

Where will I find what I need?

HINTS & TIPS

It is important to move on to development as soon as you have enough research material. Most people spend far too long on research as it can be very enjoyable!

Development

This stage of the process is where you create your own ideas in response to the brief. It is best to tackle this in three stages:

Initial ideas	• Consider a number of different possibilities – remember to work from your research and investigation material • Generate rough ideas – these can be drawings or 3D mock-ups or samples

Selection of best idea	• Evaluate work done so far to see which idea is the best – remember to refer to your brief • Select the best idea for further development

Development and refinement of selected idea	• Experiment with changes • Explore techniques and materials • Refine the idea to make improvements – reflect on your brief as you work to make sure you stay on track

Design solution

Your design solution should show your finished concept. Although you are not expected to achieve a professional finish at this level, you should aim for the best quality possible so that your idea is communicated clearly.

A poorly executed outcome will affect your final mark, so it is worthwhile taking time to plan and to select appropriate materials. You do not need to use expensive materials or processes, but if resources are very limited you should consider this at the design brief stage. This will ensure that you don't attempt something that you don't have the resources or level of skill to carry out successfully.

HINTS & TIPS

In 3D design projects, it is good practice to show some 3D development. To gain maximum marks, you should produce a carefully made 3D solution or a good quality illustration showing all the important aspects of the design.

COMMON MISTAKES

Sometimes in graphic design Portfolios, design solutions are just direct copies of one of the developments printed in a bigger format. You should ensure that your outcome shows further improvement and refinement or it will be difficult to award you maximum marks.

Evaluating design work

The general information given in the section entitled 'Evaluating Expressive Work' also applies here.

What should I evaluate in my Design Activity?

The design process

The effectiveness of the solution

COMMON MISTAKES

Once students start designing, they often forget what their brief was and end up going off in a different direction. This can cause problems if the Portfolio ends up looking confused and lacking coherence, and marks can be lost. Reviewing and evaluating your work against your design brief on a regular basis will avoid this.

BASIC AND DESCRIPTIVE COMMENT	EVALUATIVE COMMENT
Autumn leaves were the source of inspiration for my textile design unit. **Explain why.**	I chose autumn leaves as the source of inspiration for my textile design unit as I liked the warm colour scheme. I felt the shapes and the patterns would be good to develop for textiles.
This is my favourite idea. **Why?**	This idea relates best to the aims of my brief and it is the most aesthetically pleasing. I plan to develop it further in my Portfolio.
My design solution is a bit untidy. **Why, what happened?**	My solution was a bit rushed as I didn't manage my time particularly well at the development stage. In future, I would leave myself more time to finish my work to a higher standard.
My solution fulfils the design brief. **In what way?**	The chair is suitable for the target market as the futuristic style would appeal to young city apartment dwellers. It is designed to fit the human body, so would be comfortable. The design is suitable for mass production so this would keep the cost down. The chair can be stacked, which was an important aspect of the brief.

How your Design Unit relates to your Portfolio

Design Unit work

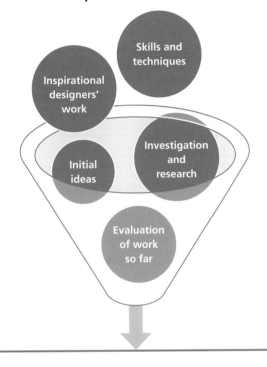

Portfolio

Selection of the **best idea** for further development

Development and refinement of this idea to solve the design brief

Exploration of appropriate techniques and materials

Reflection on effectiveness of developments

Making of final design solution/prototype

Evaluation of the solution in terms of how well it fulfils the brief

Presentation of work for external assessment

Unit

The Unit is marked on a pass or fail basis

Your Unit work will be retained in school for internal assessment

Portfolio

36 marks available for investigation and research

36 marks for the solution

8 marks for evaluation

Your finished Portfolio will be submitted to SQA for external assessment

National 4

Your work does not need to be sent to SQA for external assessment so you do not need to present it as a Portfolio. Your teacher will advise you on what format your work should be for internal assessment.

Your design solution is an important part of your Added Value Unit, which you need to complete to achieve your course award.

Use the checklist on this page to help you keep track of your Design Activity and ensure that you meet the assessment standards. You may find that your teacher will help you with the presentation or labelling of your work, or you may be required to do this yourself.

DESIGN ACTIVITY CHECKLIST

	Task	Success criteria	✓
1	Design brief	My brief is clear and easy to understand.	
		It contains information on the functional issues of the design problem.	
		It gives me direction on aesthetics (look, style, inspiration).	
		It includes information about the target market/audience/client.	
2	Research	I have evidence representing my visual inspiration (e.g. theme/style).	
		I have Critical Studies work to prove that I have learned about a range of designers/design movements related to my area of design (including at least one contemporary designer).	
		From my Critical Studies, I have selected and analysed works by at least two designers whose style/technique relate to my own Design Activity.	
		I have research on my target market.	
		I have explored the functional aspects of my design brief.	
		I have included annotations to explain my thoughts and decisions.	
3	Development	I have completed a range of initial ideas which demonstrate different responses to my brief.	
		I have explored relevant materials and/or techniques.	
		I have selected the most successful idea for further development.	
		I have produced a range of further developments based on this one idea, exploring it through adapting and refining it with reference to the requirements of the brief.	
		I have explored suitable materials and/or techniques in developing my selected idea.	
		I have evaluated my work and added annotation to explain my thoughts and decisions.	
4	Design solution	I have planned the production of my solution, taking account of the time, resources and skills required.	
		I have produced my design solution to the best standard I am capable of.	
		If appropriate (for 3D work), I have photographed my design solution, or arranged for it to be photographed.	
		I have evaluated my design solution, referring to the requirements of my original brief.	
5	Portfolio presentation	I have discussed the most suitable presentation format and style with my teacher, considering shape and size of card/paper and colour scheme.	
		I have selected all the *relevant* work from my Design Activity which demonstrates my progress towards the design solution.	
		I have arranged my work into a suitable layout and checked this with my teacher before proceeding.	
		I have carefully and neatly stuck down my work, including my design solution, or photographs of my solution.	
		I have added titles/sub-headings, where appropriate, to my work so that the design process is clear.	
		Evaluation of my research and development work is included in the form of annotations.	
		I have included evaluation of my design solution in an appropriate format.	
		The separate sheets of my Portfolio have been securely taped together on the back.	
		The labels supplied by SQA have been stuck onto the back of my Portfolio.	
	Well done – you've made it!		

'Berries and cherries'

GRAPHIC DESIGN CASE STUDY

3

Design brief

Emily has been asked to write a design brief for a packaging unit for a healthy fruit-based drink.

Emily's first attempt at writing her brief looked like this:

'I am going to design a label which has fruit images on it. I really like cherries. It should be bright and colourful. The target audience is for 5–50 year olds.'

Teacher's feedback

Good start, Emily. You need to consider a suitable client. You should also consider:

- **Purpose?** Think about this issue.
- **Target Audience/Market?** Health-conscious teenagers and their parents? Where is it to be sold?
- **Who is the client?** A new drinks company?
- **Colour & Style?** This should appeal to your target audience.
- **Imagery?** What sources of inspiration will you use?
- **Text?** Think about appropriate **style** and **size**.
- **Design Requirements?** e.g. bar code, volume capacity.

Emily's second attempt

'The drinks company "Squeeze" has commissioned me to design packaging for their new range of drinks based on fruit juice. These drinks will be marketed as an alternative to the fizzy drinks bought by teenagers. They are to be sold in supermarkets nationwide.

The packaging will need to appeal to teenagers and their parents and this should be reflected in the colour and style used. Text should be an appropriate font and size.

The imagery used should reflect the ingredients of the product.

I must include the following: bar code and volume capacity.'

Teacher's feedback

Fantastic! You now have all the information you need to get started.

Emily's spidergram

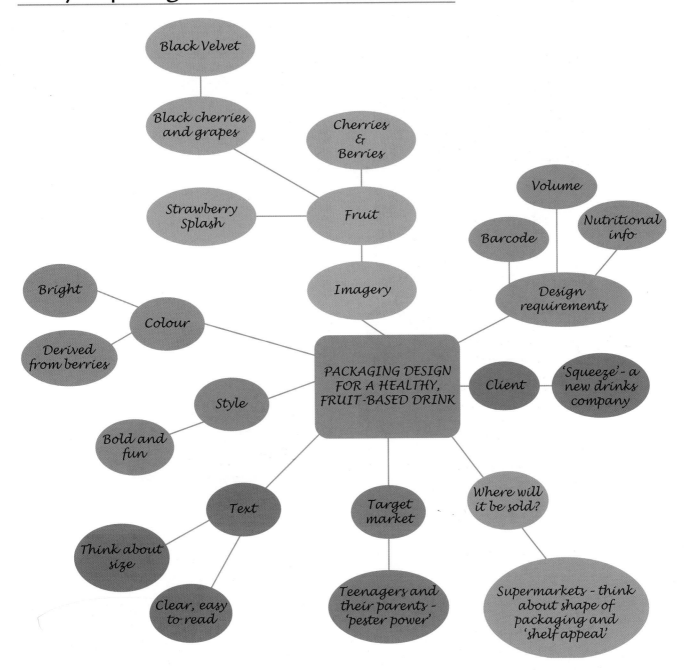

Emily has produced a spidergram to help her sort out the different aspects of her design brief. This has given her some direction for the next stage of her unit.

HINTS & TIPS

Try to be open-minded at this stage. A spidergram should help clarify your thinking, but should not restrict your creativity. If you don't like spidergrams, try writing the information as a list.

Investigation and research

Emily found that the words from her spidergram gave her inspiration and were an important part of the investigation and research process. Emily's school begins with drawings relating to the design brief, so the spidergram gave her direction when she was searching for inspirational images and photographs. She tried to source images which she could develop in her initial ideas.

Emily was told that part of her investigation should be market research. It was important for her to find what was out there in terms of existing products and what contemporary graphic designers were producing. Emily's unit work gave her the opportunity to explore a whole range of images, market research and techniques.

How Emily gathered her research

Emily found research materials on the internet, in books, at the library, in magazines and by collecting existing examples of packaging.

She found drawing was also a good method of understanding the visual qualities of her inspirational images and this allowed her to investigate the qualities of line, form, colour, pattern and shape.

HINTS & TIPS

Although it is not a requirement to produce expressive drawings in your Design Unit, it can be very helpful when you are trying to develop original ideas and a personal response to the brief. However, these do not have to be observational studies like you would produce for an Expressive Unit. Drawings for designs have a different purpose.

Market research

motif

wallpaper

Emily's teacher told her that it was important to explore all options at this stage. The more information that she could find, the more it would help her in the long term to produce interesting ideas.

Emily used the internet to gather market research images. She used a search engine, entering key words related to her brief. She used a variety of different terms. When she found an image she liked Emily clicked on it and viewed it on the actual web page. This meant she could save it as a larger image. It also gave her the opportunity to see the other images available or to follow possible links. When Emily started to exhaust the possibilities with packaging design, she extended her search into related areas such as wallpaper, pattern, motifs and logos.

contextual research

HINTS & TIPS

Ensure that all of your research is relevant to the design brief.

Initial ideas

Emily tried different approaches to line drawing. She developed work in her sketchbook by experimenting with a variety of techniques, mixing and matching techniques that she liked. She started simplifying and stylising her images, beginning with simple line drawings of fruit. She then experimented with separating the shapes in her drawings. The quality of Emily's pen work is very precise and she uses a variety of line weights. She experimented with some of the techniques below:

- continuous line
- double line drawing
- positive/negative
- adding pattern
- simplifying the shapes
- repeating the shapes
- overlapping
- zooming in
- changing the colour
- silhouette

HINTS & TIPS

At this stage, you should begin to produce lots of ideas. Don't worry about how well you draw at this point because it will hinder you in coming up with new ideas. You can always redraw the best concepts later.

Emily decided on a key image to develop further for her Portfolio.

'I really loved the circular pattern that I created to represent grapes. This was inspired by the Art Deco poster I studied in my critical activity.'

HINTS & TIPS

To experiment, you can try repeating your motifs. Try a variety of backgrounds and colours. Experiment with different sizes and layouts.

Critical studies

Pivolo (1924) by A. M. Cassandre

Emily spent time in her critical studies lessons researching graphic designers. She studied the styles and techniques of the designers which related to her own work. She enjoyed this aspect of the course because there were many designers' work she did not select for further study, but which nevertheless helped her develop personal approaches.

Emily decided to study Art Deco design in more depth as she became interested in the geometric shapes typical of this design movement. This inspired her to experiment with simple repeat shapes and to create her own geometric motifs. The limited colour palette of the Art Deco graphic designer A. M. Cassandre inspired her, and she loved his use of bold shapes. She learnt that Cassandre was known for his 'anchoring' technique, which involved connecting the image to the lettering. Emily found this useful in her packaging developments.

Related designers

Historical: This could be from design movements such as Art Nouveau, Art Deco, Bauhaus.

Contemporary: There are many young and modern designers.

Craft: Often crafts people have a different approach to design, e.g. scrap booking.

Critical studies research

Emily found that her Art & Design department had an excellent selection of books on graphic design which was helpful for researching designers' work.

Fruit Store (1941) Fruit Art Project

Eat Fruit Be Healthy (1938)
Fruit Art Project

Text development for the Portfolio

Black Velvet

Black Velvet

Black Velvet

black velvet

Black Velvet

BLACK

VELVET

Black Velvet

Black Velvet

Black Velvet

Black Velvet

BLACK

VELVET

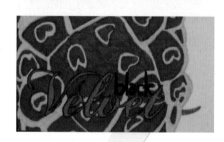

HINTS & TIPS

You can experiment with text using a light box or by taping your work to a window. Trace some of your text in different layouts and styles. You can then add your colour scheme into the letters. You could also try experimenting with pattern.

Emily spent time on the computer experimenting with different fonts. She considered:

- size
- italics
- bold
- font style

She found this way of developing ideas very quick and useful. She experimented with outline fonts, which she filled with her grapes and blackberries designs that she had previously scanned into the computer. She also tried this technique on the light box. Finally, Emily began to incorporate her text ideas and images together.

Design development

Emily went on to explore her packaging ideas by developing labels for bottles. She decided that the bottle developments were more interesting than the carton format because they were more complicated in shape. She further developed her concept by producing a multi-pack design for holding four bottles of juice.

Design solution for the Portfolio

Emily's evaluation of her final design solution

'The solution appeals to the target audience because the design is sophisticated and the colour palette will attract the older teenage target market. The bottle label is fit for purpose as it includes all of the important information and design requirements, such as a bar code. The design reflects the contents of the juice but in an original way. The repeating motif is eye-catching, yet simple and elegant. The colour palette reflects the juice ingredients.

I like the design differences between the multi-pack and the bottle label. They coordinate well, but are designed to suit their own individual purposes. If I had more time, I would have liked to experiment further with this concept.

One modification would be to include nutritional information.'

'Embroidery & embellishment'

3

- Design brief
- Initial sampling
- Initial concept designs
- Corset development
- Design solution

Design brief

Fashion/Textiles Design Brief Worksheet			
Name: Amy		**Class:** S4	

Which of the following items do you intend to design?		
Bag	Wrap	Fabric cuff
Cushion	Customised T-shirt	Fabric neckpiece
Skirt	(Corset)	Fabric corsage
The department will supply you with a basic pattern which you can adapt.		

Identify your source of inspiration	
(Natural)	Manmade
Use this space to list some possibilities:	

Snakes, geometric pattern, fashion, animal pattern and fabric manipulation.

Final decision: *To design and make a corset*

Identify your target market

Gender:		Age group:		Personal style:	
Male		Teenage	25+	Stylish	Quirky
(Female)		18–25	30+	Funky	Classic
Unisex		(20–30)	Mature	Fashion conscious	Avant-garde
		20+		Edgy	(Arty)
				Vintage	Punk

Designer influences

Historical		Contemporary	
Victoriana		Zandra Rhodes	
Art Nouveau		Vivienne Westwood	
(Art Deco)	*Erté*	(Alexander McQueen)	
Bauhaus	*Coco Chanel*	Johnathan Saunders	
60s – Biba, Pierre Cardin		Louise Gray	
70s		Holly Fulton	
80s – Steven Sprouse		Eiko Ishioka	

Materials and equipment required

(Paper)	(Fabric)	(Sewing machine)	(Needles/Pins etc)
(Recycled material)	(Bondaweb)	(Felting machine)	Wet felting equipment
Plastic bags	Dissolvable Vilene	(Iron)	(Beads/Sequins)
(Thread)	(Embroidery threads)	T-shirt	Eyelets

Skills development required

Pattern cutting	Making templates	(Hand sewing)	(Machine sewing)
(Beading)	Felt-making	(Applique)	Using heat gun
Hand dyeing	(Machine embroidery)	Making tassels/fringes	(Fabric manipulation)
Laminating/Lamifix			

Supported study workshops

Supported study is recommended – you will make more progress.
NOTE: If you have chosen to design a corset or a skirt, you **must** attend these workshops in order to make your basic garment.

Amy developed her design brief from a worksheet given to her by her class teacher. She took this information and created her own personalised design brief.

Inspired by Erté's work, Amy decided to focus on animal patterns, specifically snakeskin.

'I am going to design a corset for a special occasion. The client would like the garment to be eye-catching and unique. The corset is for a professional female who is 30 years old. The client likes Art Deco fashion but requires a modern twist. The client requires the garment to be embellished and embroidered. She likes decorative costume design.

The corset needs to be fitted and to have detailing that can be seen from a distance.'

Initial sampling for the Portfolio

From 'Drawn to Stitch' by Gwen Hedley

organic shapes

Amy developed two initial ideas for corset designs. These were developed as quick fashion drawings in her sketchbook. One was in a black and white colour scheme and one was based on a subtle warm colour palette. It was this design that she selected to take forward in her Portfolio.

layering

stitching

cutaways

Moth Dress (2010) by Alexander McQueen

Amy developed a variety of paper techniques which she layered, overlapped tend machine stitched, and cut away areas to show the colour paper underneath. She wanted to try and develop some techniques that would have an emphasis on pattern.

Design development for the Portfolio

curvilinear

shape

Amy developed small- and large-scale circles which overlapped and draped around the body.

Amy decided not to make all the circles perfectly circular but preferred the less precise organic look of her stitched paper samples.

snakeskin

xpandaprint is an interesting technique to use to create raised circular surfaces

Corset by Stefanie Nieuwenhuyse

cutaway

Amy made drawings to explore the different shapes found in snakeskin. She then scanned a line drawing into the computer and added a limited colour palette based on one of her snakeskin images.

Amy studied Erté's work. She liked the Art Deco period in terms of finishes such as snakeskin and animal inspired patterns. She liked the fact that Erté used embellishment in his fashion designs. Erté was known for his decorative style.

Gold cape (1920s) by Erté

Amy wanted to develop her textile skills. She loved experimenting with texture and fabric and wanted to manipulate fabric through stitching, cutting and layering to achieve her final outcome.

Technique development for the Portfolio

Amy spent time experimenting with fabrics. She beaded samples made from different coloured fabrics. The beading added texture and highlighted the organic shapes that she previously developed.

Amy also worked on developing fabric samples. These were based on paper examples she had created in her sketchbook. During her Unit work, Amy found that by using different weights of fabric the samples were more successful.

Amy particularly liked the use of the reversed denim in one of her layered samples. Her ideas began to focus on the development of embroidery over different combinations of woven textiles. She tried hand embroidery as well as machine stitching. Amy found it easier to annotate her sketches and samples as she was producing them. This meant she could remember the techniques used and why.

Earthy colours, patterns and textures inspire the corset designs

beading

layering

Shapes stitched by linear pattern and beads added to add shimmer to the sample. This again relates well to the snakeskin theme.

embroidery

Printed fabrics layered and then stitched onto would be visually interesting and provide a nice contrast against the plain background of the corset.

Different colour combinations of the layered samples make each one completely different from one another.

Variation in sizes of the layered samples gave lots of opportunities for development.

Stitched lines over layered fabric relate well to the investigation.

then photo printed on top. This could then be distressed with a heat gun to create a transparent effect on the fabric.

HINTS & TIPS

To achieve success with fabric samples it is necessary to experiment with textile techniques. There is a lot of information in books and on the internet to help you. You should also select fabrics in a limited colour palette that relates to your inspiration.

Design solution for the Portfolio

Amy's Art & Design department specialised in fashion and textiles. The department offered supported study evenings on textile techniques and garment construction. Amy had no experience in dressmaking or sewing before she started this project. On the advice of her teacher she made a basic corset which was easy to construct and adapt. She concentrated on making textile embellishments which were related to her developments. Amy spent a lot of time hand sewing and beading at lunchtime and after school. She would have been unable to complete this garment without this extra time, which she committed herself to at the beginning of the project.

Amy's evaluation of her final outcome

'I feel my final design meets the design requirements demanded by the brief as the corset is very unique in terms of styling, shape and detailing. My design reflects my research and development very well and it is easy to see where I got my ideas from and how they developed. I feel that I used my source of inspiration in an unusual and creative way.

I am pleased with the quality of the construction and embellishment. It is suitable for special occasions as it is decorative and the decoration can be seen from a distance, which was a requirement of the brief.

I believe that the garment would appeal to my client, a professional female aged 30. Through the embellishment, I have also achieved an Art Deco look but with a modern twist, which is what I was aiming for.

I am very pleased with my final design. However, if I could change anything I would increase the beading to add more texture to the overall corset.'

COMMON MISTAKES

Sometimes students choose to do a fashion Portfolio, but do not have the skills or the facilities to make the final outcome. While a drawing will communicate your idea to some extent, it is no substitute for a fully constructed concept garment. If you are working in fashion, it is good practice to create a 3D outcome. If you cannot do this, then a more realistic design brief might involve textile design, where you are designing the fabric only, or perhaps you could design a simpler textile item, such as a cushion or bag.

DESIGN TECHNIQUES

3

- Motif development
- Architectural development
- Paper development
- 2D and 3D development

Motif development

Some areas of design may require you to develop your own work. These may include jewellery, textiles and graphics. Design development is about making small changes and exhausting an idea. Having a limited colour palette allows you to concentrate on developing the motif through line, shape and pattern.

Sanna developed her kiwi fruit motif using design techniques such as simplifying, stylising, adding pattern, creating basic motifs and by developing repeat patterns.

She tried using different media which included collage, print-making, coloured pencil and felt-tip pen. She kept a consistent and limited colour scheme which helped unify all her design concepts.

HINTS & TIPS

Developing an idea is not always about major changes. Have fun and do not worry if there are ideas you do not like. Keep going and better ideas will happen. Design is all about development and experimentation.

Architectural development

Architectural drawing can be achieved in a number of ways. These computer-aided drawings were created using the free software program, Google Sketchup. It is simple and easy to use. By using this type of sketching method, you can see the building from a number of viewpoints and experiment with how it will look in different materials.

Sketch model-making is an excellent way to produce a mock-up of your idea. This type of model doesn't need to be highly finished. You can use paper and card and tape the pieces together. The main purpose is to help you to work out your ideas as part of your development.

You can draw your concept on a drawing board using single-point or two-point perspective to create a realistic image of your design.

Paper development

Paper mock-ups are a great method of visualising your ideas 3-dimensionally. You begin by using white paper and create your concepts by folding, cutting, layering and manipulating your paper into a design. You will find that creating your 3D idea in this way will help solve problems such as fit, function and construction.

Remember, if you cannot make your idea in paper or card, you may struggle in any other material. During this process your ideas will change – this is called development.

HINTS & TIPS

You could use acrylic paint, spray paint or tissue paper to achieve a good-quality finish.

By completing paper developments in the early stages of the design process, you can then experiment with a variety of finishes to create the aesthetic appeal that suits your design brief. Paper can be treated in different ways to give convincing finishes which can be used to produce final outcomes. It can be made to look like metal, plastic or leather, for example.

2D to 3D development

Simplified 2D shapes can be developed into 3D structures by intersecting the shapes together.

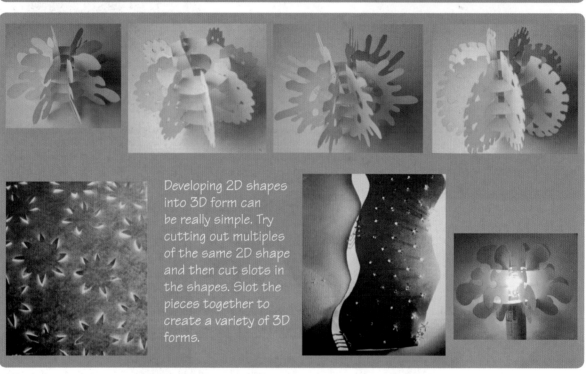

Developing 2D shapes into 3D form can be really simple. Try cutting out multiples of the same 2D shape and then cut slots in the shapes. Slot the pieces together to create a variety of 3D forms.

Paper mock-ups help solve a number of design problems, from function to style.

3D paper forms can then be developed into designs using a number of other materials.

Chapter 4

The Question Paper

The Question Paper is worth 20% of the overall mark. Your score can make the difference between a pass and a fail, or between one grade and another, so it is well worth putting in the effort to prepare for the Question Paper to maximise your mark. If you find this kind of work challenging, there are skills and techniques you can learn to help you. The time allocation for the paper is **1 hour 10 minutes**.

Structure of the Question Paper

Section 1 Art Studies
- **Q1** – You **must** answer this question. Your answer should be based on **two** artworks that you have studied.
- **Q2–Q6** – Choose **one** question from the selection. Select the question you feel most confident about answering.

Section 2 Design Studies
- **Q7** – You **must** answer this question. Your answer should based on **two** designs that you have studied.
- **Q8–Q12** – Choose **one** question from the selection. You should select the design category you are most familiar with.

Mark breakdown of the Question Paper

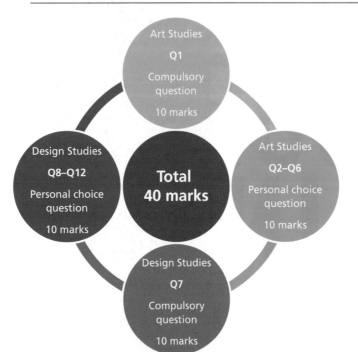

National 4

You are not required to sit a Question Paper.

You will be assessed on your Critical Studies within your Expressive and Design Units.

The information in this section will be helpful to you when you are studying the work of artists and designers in your Units.

Time management in the exam

You have **1 hour 10 minutes** in which to complete the Question Paper. This means that you have a few minutes to read the paper and decide on your personal choice questions. You should then spend around **15 minutes** on each answer, perhaps a little longer on the compulsory questions Q1 and Q7, if you have time.

Exam technique

In Critical Studies, many issues affect each other. For instance, when discussing materials, you can comment on how the choice of materials affects the style of a design. When explaining an artist's technique, you could discuss how colour is applied, and so on. The example questions and answers in this chapter should help you to develop your exam technique and learn how to respond effectively to the questions asked.

Preparing for the Question Paper

There are a number of techniques that will help you to prepare for the exam:

Try making up your own questions and marking schemes. This is a great way to understand the format of the paper and the terminology used in questions. Get a friend to do the same. You can swap questions to test each other.

Revise the meanings of Art & Design terms. You could create visual flashcards. Think about how you might illustrate the words *tone* or *perspective*, for instance.

Practise!

Work by yourself or with a friend to map out or list possible responses to questions. Challenge yourself to write down as many relevant points as you can within a time limit.

Start with some basic descriptive statements and add explanations and justifications. How would you extend the point *'this painting has been created using bright colours'*, for example?

COMMON MISTAKES

A lot of candidates think that reading through notes is an effective way to study. For most students, this approach does not work and is a very poor way to prepare for an exam. It is important that you try to learn in an 'active' way. This means using methods like those suggested above and practising as much as you can.

HINTS & TIPS

Start each answer on a new page. This means that if you have time at the end of the exam, you can revisit earlier questions and add to them. Don't forget to number your answers to indicate which personal choice questions you have attempted.

Section 1: Expressive art studies

Question 1: Expressive art studies compulsory question

These questions test your knowledge and understanding of the artworks you have studied as part of your Expressive Unit.

In this question, you will:

- Select **two** artworks by different artists who have worked on the same subject matter and/or theme

- Compare how **three** elements (specified in the question) have been used to create these artworks

- Give an opinion (stating **two** reasons for your opinion) on an aspect specified in the question

HINTS & TIPS

You cannot predict what will come up in the exam as the content of the questions will change from year to year. Therefore, it is recommended that you have a knowledge of several works of art so that you are able to respond to any question.

You will also be asked to select one artist from part (a) and explain the impact of social, cultural and/or other influences on any of their work and practice.

Expressive art issues you may be asked about in this question include:

Composition or arrangement	arrangement; pose (in figure and portrait work); setting; viewpoint; focal point; choice of subject matter; perspective; proportion; scale and use of space
Subject matter or imagery	choice of subject matter; sources of inspiration and influences; effect on the work
Visual elements	line; tone; colour; shape; form; texture; pattern; how they have been combined/applied; their effect on the work
Media handling and techniques	choice of media and processes; application of media; effect on style; treatment of subject matter; level of detail; expressive qualities; skills demonstrated; 2D or 3D; scale of the work; influences on technique
Style	aims and influence of specific art movements; what makes the work distinctive; sources of inspiration; the artists' 'trademarks'; artists' response to the subject
Scale	the dimensions of the work; large or small; effect of scale on the work; effect of scale on detail/realism/visual impact etc.
Mood and atmosphere	the mood and atmosphere created and how this has been achieved (e.g. colour, use of media, subject matter, composition, style etc.); what the work communicates to you and why

Question 1 examples

a) This question will generally begin in the same way:

(b)

Artists communicate and express their ideas about their subject in a variety of ways. Identify **two** works by different artists that you have studied. These should be based on similar **subject matter** and/or the same **theme**.

With reference to these works in your answer:

> **(b)** Select one artist from part (a). Explain the impact of social, cultural and/or other influences on any of their work and practice. **5 marks**

You will find that each year, the next part of the question will vary:

Example A

Compare each artist's use of

- composition or arrangement
- colour
- style

Which of the two works do you find most appealing? Give **two** reasons.

Total marks   10

Example B

Compare each artist's use of

- media handling and/or technique
- scale
- mood and atmosphere

Which of the two works is most effective at communicating the subject or theme? Give **two** reasons.

Total marks   10

Example C

Compare each artist's use of

- composition or arrangement
- line
- mood and atmosphere

Which of the two works is your personal favourite? Give **two** reasons.

Total marks   10

Example D

Compare each artist's use of

- subject matter and/or imagery
- media handling and/or technique
- pattern

Which of the two works is the most interesting? Give **two** reasons.

Total marks   10

Example E

Compare each artist's use of

- composition or arrangement
- colour
- texture

Which of the two works has the most creative approach? Give **two** reasons.

Total marks   10

HINTS & TIPS

It is important that you know about a variety of artworks, with different key visual elements.

You could look at artworks where line is an important element, artworks that use pattern etc.

Look at works of different scales, styles, media and techniques. That way, you should be able to respond to anything that might come up in the Question Paper.

Question 1 example answers

Response to example A

Emily's first attempt – a basic response	Teacher's notes
Two works by different artists I have studied are 'Le Vase Paille' by Paul Cezanne, painted in 1895, and 'Still Life Looking towards Stromboli and Panarea' by Leon Morrocco, which is a contemporary painting.	Explain what they have in common – theme? subject?
Cezanne's painting consists of a group of objects and fruit on a table top. There is also a vase and a tablecloth. Morrocco's painting also shows fruit on a tabletop but is set on a beach. There are two plates of fruit and what looks like a patterned cloth. There is also a small figure to the side of the table.	This is very descriptive. Use the key words in the question in your response and show your knowledge of art terms that we have covered in class. Refer to the wordbanks.
The paintings are different styles but both artists use distortion.	In what way?
The colour in Cezanne's painting is dull as there is a lot of brown. Morrocco's painting is much brighter. There is a lot of blue because of the sea behind the table.	Use your knowledge of colour theory to explain more effectively how colour is used
The work I find the most appealing is the Leon Morrocco still life. This is because it has bright colours and includes the sea.	You have given two reasons but you will not be given marks for points you have already made. We will do some more work in class to prepare for this question. Some paired work will help you tackle these questions more effectively. Consider using sub-headings to ensure that you answer all aspects of the question in depth.

HINTS & TIPS

If you only write descriptive comments you will not be answering the question fully. You are unlikely to gain maximum marks for this.

Emily's next attempt – a more in-depth and effective response	Marks

Two works by different artists I have studied are 'Le Vase Paille' by Paul Cezanne, painted in 1895 and 'Still Life Looking towards Stromboli and Panarea' by Leon Morrocco, which is a contemporary painting. They are both still life paintings of fruit and objects arranged on table tops.

Composition

Cezanne's painting has a triangular composition with a vase at the apex of the triangle. The sides of the triangle are suggested by the perspective of the tabletop. For me, this makes the vase the focal point of the painting. The background is plain, with textural brushstrokes which do not distract too much from the objects. The perspective is unusual with the tabletop tilted towards the viewer and items placed off the horizontal and vertical. Cezanne was known for altering perspective. Morrocco's painting also experiments with perspective, which is flattened even more than in Cezanne's. The table is set against a background of sky and sea. There is also a small figure to the side of the table and a boat which, along with the horizon line, helps give the painting distance and depth. I would say there is no one focal point to this busy painting, as my eye tends to wander around the composition from object to object.

(✓ ✓ ✓ ✓ ✓)

Colour

Cezanne's colour palette is mainly warm tertiary colours, but these are balanced in places with jewel-like greens, yellows and oranges. The drab background helps keep my attention on the fruit.

(✓)

Morrocco's painting is much brighter with saturated colours. The painting is dominated by the cold blue background but is balanced by the warm pink tabletop and the hot colours of the fruit.

(✓)

Style

The paintings are different styles but both artists use distortion. Cezanne's distorted perspective was a key part of his Post-Impressionist style, as he was not concerned with painting reality but with creating balance and harmony in his work.

(✓)

The artists both use oil paint but applied in a different way. Cezanne uses directional brushstrokes and broken outlines. Paint is applied in thin transparent layers to build up the colour. Cezanne would sometimes take months or even years to finish a painting as he was a perfectionist constantly striving for harmony.

(✓ ✓)

Morrocco's painting has flatter, more opaque colour, but has textural areas here and there. He uses bolder outlines than Cezanne.

(✓)

The painting I find most appealing is the Morrocco still life. I love its vibrant colour which reminds me of hot sunny days. The subject matter and the background of blue sky and sea give me happy memories of being on holiday.

(✓ ✓)

You have made more than 10 valid justified points and answered all aspects of the question. Good use of art terminology. The group work tasks in class have really helped your exam technique. Well done!

10

Response to example C

Beth's response	Marks
Two works by different artists I have studied are 'Weeping Woman' by Pablo Picasso, painted in 1937, and 'The Troubled City' by Ken Currie, painted in 1991. Both paintings are responses to the theme of conflict.	
Composition	
Picasso's painting is a portrait, concentrating on a head and shoulders. It is not always clear with Picasso which way the subject is facing as he uses multiple viewpoints. This can be seen in this painting as the subject appears to be facing us, but is in side profile at the same time. The woman appears to be in a room, which is suggested by the shapes in the background. The focal point of this painting is the subject's eyes, which remind me of broken and shattered windows.	✓ ✓
Ken Currie's painting is a figure composition and is very complex. It is a large crowd scene with a tangle of figures receding all the way to the background, which appears to be burning buildings. The ladder being carried creates a vertical line which leads your eye to the figure with the megaphone, which for me is the focal point.	✓ ✓
Line	
Lines are used to outline and emphasise the jagged geometric shapes in Picasso's painting. The hair is also simplified and depicted with bold lines. This is typical of Picasso's Cubist style, where objects are represented through line and shape. This technique flattens the perspective.	✓ ✓ ✓
In Currie's painting, outlines are often blurred and indistinct, which gives the impression of figures dissolving into the shadows. This helps to add to the confusion of the scene.	✓
Mood and atmosphere	
Both paintings have very different styles but, as both depict conflict, they both convey a disturbing atmosphere. Picasso's painting was about the Spanish Civil War and this suggests that the woman is mourning or grieving for someone lost, or perhaps about what is happening to Spain. This is shown by the fact that she is holding a handkerchief to her face and by the expressive colour and shapes used.	✓ ✓ ✓
I am not sure what the conflict is about in Currie's painting, but it also suggests civil war with rioting and looting. The skull-like faces of the figures and their decaying flesh suggests death and portrays a dark, sinister atmosphere. The burning city and weapons being carried by many of the figures suggest destruction and violence.	✓ ✓ ✓
I like both paintings but my personal favourite is by Ken Currie. Although it is distressing to look at, it shows conflict in a very graphic way. His style of painting with its sombre colours and deep, dark tones helps to convey the horrors of war.	✓ ✓
More than 10 justified points have been made and all aspects of the question have been answered. It is clear that you understand the key points about the paintings. An excellent personal response!	10

Questions 2–6: Expressive art studies personal choice question

You will choose **one question** to answer from this selection. This part of the Question Paper is all about responding to an unseen image. You will be applying what you have learned in your Critical Studies. The marker will expect to see you demonstrate knowledge and understanding of art practice and to be able to apply terminology correctly.

Each question has a related image. These will change from year to year, but you can get an idea of the variety likely to come up by looking at SQA's specimen Question Paper and past papers. You can also prepare for this part of the paper by trying to broaden your experience of art in general.

Once you have read through this section, along with the worked examples, have a go at answering the questions. There are no 'right answers', but your responses should show a knowledge and understanding of Critical Studies.

You can expect to find a variety of genres and approaches in the paper, such as:

Questions 2–6 examples

Art from other cultures and times

In the Question Paper, examples of artwork from ancient times to the present day may be represented. You may also find artworks from other cultures. You will probably be familiar with Western art, but it is a good idea to look at some artworks from other cultures. This will increase your confidence in discussing less familiar artworks and will extend your choice in the exam.

Emperor Jahangir Receiving his Two Sons (1605–06) by Manohar
Gouache on paper (20.8 cm × 15.4 cm)

Example A

Artists from earlier times and other cultures often represent the world in ways that may seem unusual to us. Comment on the methods used to create this painting. In your answer, refer to:

- composition
- colour
- pattern

What is you opinion of this style of painting. Give **two** reasons.

Total marks   10

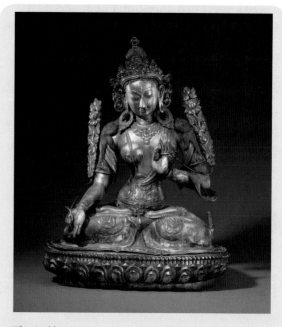

The Goddess Tara (1426–35) by an unknown artist
Bronze, gold, gilding and paint
(26.6 cm × 16.3 cm × 15 cm)

Example B

Some artists have been inspired to create representations of gods and goddesses. Comment on this example. In your answer, refer to:

- pose
- decoration
- materials

What does this sculpture communicate to you? Give **two** reasons.

Total marks   10

Response to example B

Robyn's first, descriptive response	Robyn's second, more analytical response
<u>Pose</u> The goddess is sitting cross-legged with one hand raised. She is looking downwards.	<u>Pose</u> The goddess is sitting cross-legged with one hand raised. This reminds me of a yoga position and makes her look like she is meditating. She is looking downwards which adds to the idea that she may be meditating or thinking. Her face reminds me of a Buddha.
<u>Decoration</u> There is a lot of decoration on the statue. It is sitting on a decorative base. She is wearing a crown and jewellery. There are flowers growing up and intertwining with her arms.	<u>Decoration</u> There is a lot of decoration on the statue. The goddess is covered in jewellery. There is decorative jewellery around her neck and waist, and bracelets on her wrists. She is wearing large, heavy earrings. This makes her look rich and opulent. She is wearing a very ornate crown which makes her seem important. The style of the clothing and jewellery looks Eastern or oriental. There are flowers growing up and intertwining with her arms. This makes her look like she is connected with nature in some way. The statue is sitting on a very decorative base. It reminds me of a scallop shell and reinforces the idea that the goddess is something to do with nature.
<u>Materials</u> The statue is made of bronze and gold with gilding and paint.	<u>Materials</u> The statue is made of bronze, and although it is a small statue it will be quite heavy. The shiny, gold finish reminds me of royalty as I associate this colour with wealth and status. The attention to detail in this small sculpture is amazing and it must have been made by a very skilled artist.
<u>What it communicates to me</u> The statue does not look like a typical goddess. Try to develop these by thinking about the effect achieved and the reasons why the artist has made the sculpture like this.	<u>What it communicates to me</u> The statue does not look like a typical goddess as I am used to the idea of classical Greek or Roman goddesses. The Goddess Tara, with her peaceful expression, looks as if she is a kind and caring goddess. Excellent response!

HINTS & TIPS
Generally, you will be awarded one mark for each well-justified point made which is relevant to the question being asked. Remember that you will need to respond to all aspects of the question to gain full marks.

Sculpture and site-specific art

The Family Group (1949) by Henry Moore
Bronze (154 cm × 118 cm × 70 cm)

Example C

Artists have always been inspired by the human form. Comment on how the artist has responded to this subject. In your answer, refer to:

■ arrangement
■ form
■ style

What mood does this work suggest to you? Give **two** reasons.

Total marks   10

Touchstone North (1990) by Andy Goldsworthy
Stone

Example D

The natural world is a source of inspiration for many artists. Comment on how this artist has responded to the natural environment. In your answer, refer to:

■ arrangement
■ shape and/or form
■ materials

What is your opinion of this approach to sculpture? Give **two** reasons.

Total marks   10

Flying Pins (2000) by Claes van Oldenburg
and Coosje van Bruggen
Steel, fibre-reinforced plastic, PVC foam, painted with polyester gelcoat and polyurethane enamel
(Each pin is 7.5 m high)

Example E

Large sculptures are sometimes made for public places.

Comment on this sculpture.

In your answer, refer to:

■ scale
■ arrangement
■ subject matter

What is your personal response to this sculpture? Give **two** reasons.

Total marks   10

Drawing, painting and printmaking

La Jupe Verte (*The Green Skirt*) (c.1897–1901)
by Edgar Degas
Pastel on paper (45 cm × 37 cm)

Example F

Artists often use drawing as a way of recording what they see. Comment on the methods used by the artist to capture this scene. In your answer, refer to:

■ composition
■ line
■ colour

How successful is this technique?
Give **two** reasons.

Total marks   10

Sandwich and Soda (1964) by Roy Lichtenstein
Screenprint on acetate (48.5 cm × 58.4 cm)

Example G

Everyday subjects are a source of inspiration for many artists. Comment on the artist's approach to the subject matter in this print. In your answer, refer to:

■ composition
■ colour
■ shape

What is your opinion of this style of work?
Give **two** reasons.

Total marks   10

Head of a Woman (15th century)
by Andrea del Verrocchio
Chalk on paper (32.5 cm x 27.2 cm)

Example H

Often artists use drawing to create studies for paintings. Comment on this portrait study. In your answer, refer to:

■ composition
■ line
■ tone

What does this work communicate to you?
Give **two** reasons.

Total marks   10

Response to example H

Sanna's response	Marks
<u>Composition</u> 'Head of a Woman' by Andrea del Verrocchio is a portrait study. The composition is unusual in that it is closed in, concentrating only on the head. The subject is gazing downwards. In most portraits I have seen, the subject is looking at the viewer. This makes the subject appear shy. Her head is tilted to one side and the viewpoint is a three-quarter profile rather than facing straight on. This also adds to the idea that she is turning away from the artist and is self-conscious.	✓ ✓ ✓
<u>Line</u> Line has been used very sensitively and the artist must have had a very high level of skill to be able to draw like this. Line is used to define the features, but it is soft and not heavy and used in a delicate way. There is great attention to detail, with every line in the hair carefully drawn. The artist seems to have been particularly interested in the girl's hair style, which appears to be drawn more precisely than the rest of the study. Every detail of the plaits has been picked out in line.	✓ ✓ ✓ ✓
<u>Tone</u> Tone has been used to suggest form and to model the features of the girl's face. Shadows and highlights have been depicted and the tone is softly blended. A wide tonal range has been used, from very dark to very light, and this helps to give the drawing a sense of realism.	✓ ✓
What this drawing communicates to me is that it was probably a study for a painting. Many artists make drawings before they attempt a finished piece and I think that is what has happened here. I think the girl was probably posing for the artist in this way, so that she could be included in a larger painting later.	✓ ✓
This is an excellent response. I like how you have demonstrated you knowledge of artists' methods in the conclusions, rather than just repeating points already made.	10

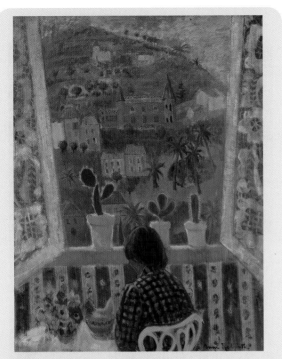

Window in Menton (1948) by Anne Redpath
Oil on plywood (109.2 cm × 83.8 cm)

Example I

Many artists have been inspired by their travels. Comment on this artist's response to the subject matter. In your answer, refer to:

- composition
- colour
- pattern

What mood and atmosphere does this painting communicate to you?
Give **two** reasons.

Total marks   10

The Aviary, Clifton (1888) by Joseph Crawhall
Watercolour on paper (51 cm × 35 cm)

Example J

The subject of animals has interested many artists. Comment on this artist's treatment of the subject. In your answer, refer to:

- composition
- colour
- media handling

How well has the artist captured the subject matter? Give **two** reasons.

Total marks   10

Autumn in Glencairn, Moniaive (1887) by James Paterson
Oil on canvas (102 cm × 127 cm)

Example K

Artists have always been inspired to paint their surroundings. Comment on this artist's response to the landscape. In your answer, refer to the use of:

- composition
- colour
- technique

What mood and atmosphere does this painting communicate? Give **two** reasons.

Total marks   10

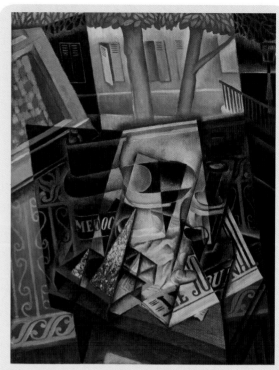

Still Life before an Open Window, Place Ravignan (1915) by Juan Gris
Oil on canvas (115.9 cm × 88.9 cm)

Example M

Many artists have experimented with new ways of representing their subjects. Comment on how the artist has responded to this still life. In your answer, refer to:

- composition
- shape
- colour

What is your opinion of this style of painting? Give **two** reasons.

Total marks   10

The Four Horsemen of the Apocalypse (1498) by Albrecht Dürer
Woodcut print on paper (39.4 cm × 28.1 cm)

Example L

Throughout history, artists have been inspired to create works of fantasy and imagination. Comment on this artist's approach. In your answer, refer to:

- composition
- line
- imagery

What mood and atmosphere does this work communicate to you? Give **two** reasons.

Total marks   10

Mixed media

Dr Tom Normand (1998) by Steven Campbell
Mixed media on canvas (182 cm × 97 cm)

Example N

Many artists have developed unusual ways of creating artwork. Comment on how the artist has approached the subject of portraiture. In your answer, refer to:

■ composition
■ colour
■ technique

What does the artist communicate about the subject of this work? Give **two** reasons.

Total marks   10

Children and Chalked Wall 3 (1962) by Joan Eardley
Oil, newspaper and metal foil on canvas
(61 cm × 68.6 cm)

Example O

Artists have often been inspired by the subject of children. Comment on the methods used to create this painting. In your answer, refer to:

■ pose
■ texture
■ colour

What does the artist communicate about the character of the children? Give **two** reasons.

Total marks   10

Response to example N

Beth's first descriptive response	Beth's second more analytical response
Composition	Composition
The subject is sitting on a tall stool. He is in a room. There is lettering spelling his name on the right-hand side. The subject is looking out of the picture.	The subject is sitting on a tall stool looking directly at the viewer. His pose is relaxed, with his legs crossed and his arms also crossed over on his knees. The setting appears to be a room. There seems to be a wall behind the subject with some pictures. The viewpoint is eye level with the subject. This is a large-scale piece suggesting the subject is life size. The perspective is quite flat but there is a sense that the stool is sitting on the floor. This is suggested by an area of lighter tone. One unusual thing about the composition is the lettering spelling his name on the right-hand side. It is arranged vertically, which mirrors the vertical line made by the subject on the other side. There is also a 'shadow' behind the subject, which is like a mirror image of the subject in silhouette.
Colour	Colour
The colours are dull. He has used browns and a dark red.	The colours are drab browns and creams with accents of a dark red. These are warm tones. The effect is of warm, neutral colours.
Technique	Technique
The artist has used mixed media. It looks as if he has used collage. There are drips of paint. I have not seen a portrait like this before. It is very unusual. Remember to use the art terms you learned about in class. You have also been taught how to analyse a composition, so look at your notes. You should also refer to your Critical Studies wordbanks to help you write a more detailed response.	The artist has used mixed media. It looks as if he has used collage. There is what appears to be a sketchbook on the floor and pictures on the walls. It looks as if these are pictures and printed papers which the artist has stuck on. Watery drips of paint have run down the canvas creating an interesting textural effect. The lettering is very flat and has a 1960s style. It also looks as if it has been cut out and stuck on. A 'halo' of white paint has been applied around the subject, which adds emphasis. The figure is painted quite realistically, but the face is slightly stylised as the eyes have been made larger than normal. This focuses your attention on his face. I have not seen a portrait like this before. It is very unusual that the subject's name has been included, especially so large. When I saw the title, I thought he looked very young to be a doctor, but the painting suggests that he is a person at ease with himself. Much better response!

Photography

Migrant Mother (c.1936) by Dorothea Lange
Gelatin-silver print (38 cm × 49 cm)

Example P

Photographers sometimes capture images which help to tell a story. Comment on the photographer's response to this scene. In your answer, refer to:

■ composition
■ subject matter
■ lighting

What mood and atmosphere is conveyed by the image? Give **two** reasons.

Total marks   10

Example Q

Photographs capture a moment in time. Comment on the approach used to create this image. In your answer, refer to:

■ camera angle
■ shape
■ tone

How well has the photographer captured the mood of the event? Give **two** reasons.

Total marks   10

Big Cycling Race, Madison Square Garden New York (1932) by Fred Zinnemann
Gelatin-silver print (16.8 cm × 11.5 cm)

Photograph from *The Last Resort* series (1983–85) by Martin Parr

Example R

Many photographers are inspired by ordinary life. Comment on this photographer's approach. In your answer, refer to:

■ subject matter
■ composition
■ mood and atmosphere

What is your opinion of this style of photography? Give **two** reasons.

Total marks   10

Response to example Q

Jacob's response	Marks
'Big Cycling Race, Madison Square Garden, New York' by Fred Zinnemann makes use of a camera angle with a viewpoint above the subjects. This allows the photographer to look down on the race and to capture the cyclists going past at just the right moment. His angle of view means that the spectators are also in the frame. This helps to create a sense of distance, with the closer spectators in the foreground and the smaller spectators in the background giving a sense of perspective to the scene.	✓ ✓ ✓ ✓
There is a dominant curved shape created by the track, which seems to be in a velodrome as it is at a steep angle. This leads your eye into the picture and to the cyclists coming around the bend, which is the focal point of the picture. The silhouettes of the spectators who are wearing hats give an idea that this is a historical photograph without you even having to look at the date. The cyclists have an indistinct shape as they are moving. This gives a sense of speed.	✓ ✓ ✓
There is a range of tones, but the image is mainly dark as the crowd is in shadow. Only the race track is illuminated, which is another reason it is the focal point of the image. The image is high contrast, with a few midtones.	✓ ✓ ✓
I think this image captures an atmosphere of excitement. This is suggested by members of the crowd all standing up and leaning forward. It looks as if four cyclists are in the lead and it is uncertain who is going to win, which adds to the suspense of the crowd.	✓
The speed of the cyclists conveyed by the motion blur also adds to the excitement of the scene.	✓
Your answer shows a good understanding of issues relating to photography. You have written a lot of valid and well reasoned points, scoring full marks.	10

HINTS & TIPS

Remember that photography has its own terminology. It is said that photography is like 'painting with light'. You can discuss the effect of light and shade, camera angles and camera techniques on the image. Think about how the subject has been framed and whether it was 'set up' or something the photographer saw and responded to.

COMMON MISTAKES

Sometimes candidates do not read the information given about the work and respond to a photograph or a sculpture as if it were a painting, discussing paint techniques, for instance. Be careful to read the caption under the work so that you do not make this mistake.

Section 2: Design studies

Question 7: Design studies compulsory question

This question tests your knowledge and understanding of designers' work and design issues you have studied as part of your Design Unit.

In this question, you will:

- Select **two** designs by different designers who have worked in the same area of design

- Compare how **three** design issues (specified in the question) have been considered while creating these designs

- Give an opinion (stating **two** reasons for your opinion) on an aspect specified in the question

HINTS & TIPS

It is important that you have a knowledge of works by at least two designers. These designers must work in the same design area, for example, two graphic designers, two product designers, two jewellery designers, etc.

Try to find designers who have contrasting styles and approaches.

You will also be asked to select one designer from part (a) and explain the impact of social, cultural and/or other influences on any of their work and practice.

Design issues you may be asked about in the question include:

Function/Fitness for purpose	purpose; primary and secondary functions; effectiveness; durability; practicality/wearability; safety; ergonomics/user-friendliness
Aesthetics/Style	visual impact; visual elements (line, tone, colour, shape, form, texture, pattern); how visual elements have been used/combined; influences of other designers/design movements; sources of inspiration; scale; detail; decoration
Materials and techniques	choice of materials; processes used; use of technology; production/construction methods; skills demonstrated; effect on the function and appearance of the design; suitability; cost
Target market/Audience	the market/audience the design is aimed at; consumer type; client; age group; gender; income bracket; interests; preferences; personality type

Question 7 examples

Questions will generally begin in the same way:

(a)
Designers have to show creativity in their approach to developing designs.

Identify **two** designs by different designers that you have studied who have worked in the same design area.

With reference to these works in your answer:

(b) Select one designer from part (a). Explain the impact of social, cultural and/or other influences on any of their work and practice. **5 marks**

You will find that each year, the next part of the question will vary:

Example A

Compare both designs in terms of:
- function
- materials and/or techniques
- visual impact

Which of the two designs is most effective? Give **two** reasons for your answer.

Total marks   10

Example B

Compare both designs in terms of:
- fitness for purpose
- target market/audience
- style

Which of the two designs is the most appealing? Give **two** reasons for your answer.

Total marks   10

Example C

Compare both designs in terms of:
- materials and/or techniques
- fitness for purpose
- influences/sources of inspiration

Which of the two designs is the most creative? Give **two** reasons for your answer.

Total marks   10

Example D

Compare both designs in terms of:
- function
- style
- materials and/or techniques

Which of the two designs do you prefer? Give **two** reasons.

Total marks   10

Example E

Compare both designs in terms of:
- influences/sources of inspiration
- function
- target market/audience

Which of the two designs is the most suitable for its purpose? Give **two** reasons.

Total marks   10

HINTS & TIPS

As the question requires you to make a comparison, it is easier to do this with designs that have a similar purpose, for example, two chairs, two lights, two posters, two bridges, two examples of outfits for women, two neckpieces, two shoe designs, two examples of packaging, etc.

Question 7 example answers

Response to example A

Darren's first attempt – a basic response	Teacher's notes
Two product designs by different designers are the Cobweb Table Lamp by Louis Comfort Tiffany, designed around 1900, and the Anglepoise lamp by George Carwadine, designed in 1932.	
Both designs are designed to give light and illumination. One is a table lamp and the other is a desk lamp.	You need to go into more detail about their function.
The Tiffany lamp is made of stained glass and bronze. It is very detailed. The Anglepoise lamp is made of metal and a special spring, which Carwadine designed.	It isn't enough to give a list of materials – you need to discuss the effect of the materials and how they are used. You could also consider issues like cost and suitability.
The Cobweb lamp has visual impact as it is colourful and decorative. The Anglepoise lamp is more plain.	Think about how you can expand on this. Visual impact is about aesthetics – consider other aesthetic issues, such as influences and sources of inspiration.
I think the Anglepoise design is the most effective for a desk lamp, but the Cobweb lamp would make a better table lamp.	This is a valid point, but you need to explain the reasons to get the marks.

COMMON MISTAKES

Candidates often lose marks because they do not develop points made. Try to get into the habit of making a point and then adding an explanation or justification.

HINTS & TIPS

Many design issues relate to other issues. For instance, in a question about visual impact you could refer to how materials affect the appearance of the design, even though you may not have been asked about materials in the question. Do not be too literal in your interpretation of the question.

Darren's next attempt – a more in-depth and effective response	Marks
Two product designs by different designers are the Cobweb Table Lamp by Louis Comfort Tiffany, designed around 1900, and the Anglepoise lamp by George Carwadine, designed in 1932.	
Function	
Both designs give light and illumination but for different purposes. The function of the Tiffany lamp is to be used on a table to create ambient lighting in one area of a room. It also has a decorative function as it is very ornamental in style.	✓ ✓
The Anglepoise is a desk lamp which can be used for task lighting to illuminate a piece of work, for instance.	✓
Materials/Techniques	
The Tiffany lamp is made of stained glass and bronze. Each lamp was handmade using traditional techniques. The method was very time-consuming, which meant that the lamps were expensive to produce and buy. The stained glass gives a decorative effect and is very attractive when lit up. The glass material meant that the lamps were fragile and had to be cleaned and handled carefully.	✓ ✓ ✓
The Anglepoise lamp is made of metal, which is tough and durable. Carwadine designed a special spring, which meant that the lamp could be repositioned without it moving back to its original place. This meant that the lamp could be used in a variety of different positions and made it very versatile and functional. The lamps could also be mass-produced which kept the costs down.	✓ ✓ ✓
Visual Impact	
The Cobweb lamp has visual impact as it is colourful and decorative. The lamps were popular in the early 1900s for their typical Art Nouveau styling. This was when product designers were inspired by nature and organic forms.	✓
The Anglepoise lamp is more plain and industrial in appearance. Its appearance is secondary to its function. It is more like a Bauhaus design, where 'form follows function'.	✓
I think the Cobweb lamp makes the best table lamp as it creates soft, diffused lighting. However, the Anglepoise design is the most effective for a desk lamp as it can be adjusted. Both designs are classics which have stood the test of time.	✓ ✓
More than 10 justified points have been made and you have answered all aspects of the question. You have answered on each aspect very well and your answer is clearly structured. I particularly like your conclusion, as it reflects the fact that both lamps have different functions. The Mies van der Rohe 'form follows function' quote is also used well here and shows a wide knowledge of the subject.	10

Response to example E

Emily's response	Marks
Two graphic designs by different designers are 'Pivolo' by Cassandre, designed in 1924, and 'Just Do It' by Neville Brody, which is from 1988.	
Function	
Both designs are advertisements. The Cassandre design is for an alcoholic drink called 'Pivolo', and the Brody design is for the sportswear company Nike and makes use of their slogan 'Just do it'. The Cassandre design is in a conventional portrait format, suggesting it was to be used as a poster or perhaps as an advertisement in a magazine. The landscape format of the Brody design suggests it is intended to be used on a billboard.	✓ ✓ ✓ ✓
Influences/Sources of Inspiration	
The design by Cassandre is influenced by the Art Deco movement. During this movement, designs became simplified and streamlined, including graphics. The bird motif has been reduced to basic shapes, but is still instantly recognisable as a magpie. The glass has also been simplified and stylised. The lettering is geometric and colours are counter-changed, which is typical of this style.	✓ ✓ ✓
I feel that the Neville Brody design is influenced by typography. He is well known for creating his own fonts and for experimenting with typography and unconventional layouts. His early designs were created using traditional techniques but this design shows the influence of the computer and digital techniques, combining text with digital images.	✓ ✓
Target Audience	
The Cassandre design is aimed at adults who might consume the product. The poster has a 'fun' style and would have been fashionable in its day, which suggests that the target audience was young, style-conscious adults who liked to try new things.	✓
The Brody design is also aimed at a young audience, perhaps teens to early 20s. The design is split down the middle and combines photography and typography. The text runs in different directions suggesting movement, and the close-up shot of the face gives the poster a dynamic look. The choice of words, such as 'bounce' and 'slam', also helps to convey the sporty message and appeal to the young audience.	✓ ✓
I think the Brody poster requires prior knowledge of the brand, as the actual product shots are quite small and hidden among the text. For this reason, I do not think it is the most suitable for its purpose. In my opinion, the Cassandre poster is the most suitable for its purpose, as it gives a very clear message and it is obvious what is being advertised because of the prominent lettering and imagery.	✓ ✓
More than 10 justified points have been made and you have answered all aspects of the question. This is a well-constructed answer showing good understanding of the concepts. Good idea to answer on function first. Well done!	10

Questions 8–12: Design studies personal choice question

You will choose to answer **one question** from this selection. Each question has a related image.

You can expect to find questions on the following design areas in the paper:

It makes sense to select the question that relates to the area you have been covering in your Design Unit. This is because each design area has its own specialist terminology. Also, if you have been involved in a particular area of design in your own practical work, you should have a deeper understanding of the issues.

COMMON MISTAKES

Some candidates don't know the meaning of important terms, which means they don't understand the question being asked. Make sure that you revise the meaning of all important design terms and that you know the difference between aesthetics issues and functional issues, for instance.

HINTS & TIPS

When responding to questions in the exam, use the key words from the questions in your answers, so that it is clear you are answering the question being asked.

Critical analysis example questions

Graphic design

In graphic design questions, you may be asked about designs for posters, stamps, packaging, book jackets, magazine covers, leaflets and web pages.

UN Economic and Social Development stamp designs

Example A

Graphic designers often have to come up with ways of communicating messages using images and text. Comment on these stamp designs. In your answer, refer to:

■ layout
■ imagery
■ colour

How effective are these stamp designs? Give **two** reasons.

Total marks   10

Packaging design for Doves Farm cereals (2012) designed by Studio H

Example B

Graphic designers have to create designs which appeal to specific target markets. Comment on these packaging designs. In your answer, refer to:

■ imagery
■ text
■ colour

What is the target market for this packaging design? Give **two** reasons.

Total marks   10

Women of Britain poster (1941) designed by Donald Zec

Example C

Graphic designs often have to convey a message in a memorable way. Comment on the design of this poster. In your answer, refer to:

■ layout
■ text
■ imagery

How well has the designer created a poster with visual impact? Give **two** reasons.

Total marks   10

Response to example B

Sanna's response	Marks
<u>Imagery</u> The imagery used in these two co-ordinating designs for cereal packaging suggests plants and growth. The Cocoa Rice box also incorporates birds and monkeys which makes me think of the rainforest. It also gives an exotic look. The designers probably wanted to give the idea of where chocolate comes from. The Fibre Flakes box has plants you might find here, such as dandelions, as well as a butterfly. It suggests farmland. The butterfly makes you think that the product must be grown without pesticides. The imagery is stylised and simplified. It reminds me of Art Deco graphics. Both designs also have a photograph – a product shot of the cereal from a bird's eye view. This lets the consumer see what it looks like. <u>Text</u> The text is quite understated. It includes the company logo, the name of the cereal and the fact that it is gluten free. In the layout, this is all placed prominently along the top of the box so that it is easily read. The font is a classic-looking sans-serif style which co-ordinates with the imagery nicely. <u>Visual Impact</u> The colour scheme works well. Both boxes have earthy colours, which means they will look good sitting together on a supermarket shelf. The colours help give the product an identity. The brown background is an obvious choice for the chocolate-flavoured cereal. The muted colours suggest that the product is natural and does not use chemicals or additives. It makes it seem healthy. <u>Target Market</u> I think the target market for this cereal is young, health-conscious adults, as the design is quite sophisticated. It may also appeal to children because of the animals, but I don't think this is the main target market as you would expect it to be more colourful. I think the design also looks expensive, so it may appeal to those who don't mind paying extra for a luxury product.	✓ ✓ ✓ ✓ ✓ ✓ ✓ ✓ ✓ ✓ ✓ ✓ ✓
A very full answer with all personal observations and opinions well justified. Your response demonstrates a good understanding of graphic design issues. Your answer is well written and you have packed in a lot of points without repeating yourself.	10

Mark II stacking chairs (1962) by Robin Day
Injection-moulded polypropylene shell on a metal
base (73.7 cm × 53.3 cm × 41.9 cm)

Product design

In this question, you could be asked about any type of product. Possibilities include furniture, lighting, household products and technological products.

Radio in a bag (1981) by Daniel Weil
Transistor radio components in a printed plastic
PVC bag (29 cm × 20.7 cm × 3 cm)

Example D

Designers have to combine form and function to solve design problems. Comment on this chair design. In your answer, refer to:

- fitness for purpose
- style
- materials

What is the target market for these chairs? Give **two** reasons.

Total marks 10

Example E

Designers often update existing products. Comment on this design for a radio. In your answer, refer to:

- fitness for purpose
- materials
- target market

What is your opinion on the style of this radio? Give **two** reasons.

Total marks 10

Example F

Designers have to consider appearance as well as purpose. Comment on this teapot design. In your answer, refer to:

- source of inspiration
- fitness for purpose
- materials

Who might buy this teapot? Give **two** reasons.

Total marks 10

Teapot (1892) by R. & W. Sorley, Glasgow
Silver (14 cm × 21 cm × 12.7 cm)

Response to example D

Darren's first attempt – a basic response	Teacher's notes
These chairs are fit for purpose. They look functional as they stack up.	You need to respond in more detail. Think of issues that affect function.
The style is quite ordinary. You see chairs like this every day.	
They are made of an injection-moulded polypropylene shell on a metal base.	This is true, but you need to expand on this point. You won't get marks for giving information from the question without expanding on it.
I think the target market for these chairs is everyone.	Try to justify this point with two reasons.

Darren's next attempt	Marks
I think these chairs are fit for purpose. They have been cleverly designed to stack up, which will save space when they are not in use. They look comfortable, as they seem to have been moulded to fit the body and it looks as if they have an optional padded cushion, which will add to the comfort. The legs have what looks like rubber stoppers on the ends. I think this is probably so that the floor doesn't get damaged.	✓ ✓ ✓
The style is quite ordinary. You see chairs like this every day but it is surprising that these were designed in 1962, so I think they must have been ahead of their time in terms of style. The form is quite organic looking as there are no sharp edges. It is good that they appear to come in a range of colours as this will allow consumers to buy the colours that suit them best.	✓ ✓ ✓
The chairs are made of an injection-moulded polypropylene shell on a metal base. The plastic material is ideal as it is lightweight, so it will be easy to move the chairs to stack them. Plastic is waterproof and can be washed to keep it clean. This material can also be formed into any shape and is low cost, which will keep the price down. The metal legs look like tubular steel which will also help to keep the design lightweight.	✓ ✓ ✓ ✓
I think the target market for these chairs is everyone. You see them in so many places, such as schools and offices, although I think they are less likely to be used in the home as they are more functional than decorative. I have even seen small versions which can be used by primary age children.	✓ ✓
Much better, Darren! A very effective answer which covers the main points well.	10

Response to example F

Becky's first attempt – a basic response	Teacher's notes
I think this teapot looks like a thistle. It looks quite fun.	You have noticed the main source of inspiration – you just need more detail.
It looks fit for purpose but the handle might get hot.	
The teapot is made of silver, so I think it would be expensive to buy.	Good point – but what is the reason for this? Can you think of any other points? Think about how it might have been made.
I think people who like Scottish things might buy the teapot.	This is about target market – personal style, age group, gender, income bracket, etc.

Becky's next attempt	Marks
I think the source of inspiration for this teapot must have been a thistle. The form is clearly based on the shape of a thistle. There is a lot of attention to detail, with the repeating overlapping pattern found on the thistle flower worked into the surface of the teapot. This looks like diamond shapes and adds interest and decoration to the design. The handle on the lid is also a small thistle and this motif is repeated on top of the handle. The lid also seems to have been engraved with thistle leaves. Perhaps the designer wanted to make something with a Scottish theme as the thistle is our national flower.	✓ ✓ ✓ ✓
Judging by the dimensions, it is quite a small teapot, maybe just big enough for one or two cups of tea. It does look fit for purpose as the spout looks well designed and as if it would pour well. However, the handle could get hot as it is made of metal and metal conducts heat. The handle on the lid will mean that it is easier to lift, although this might get hot as well as it is made of metal.	✓ ✓ ✓
The teapot is made of silver, so I think it would be expensive to buy as this is an expensive material. The teapot looks as if it has been made by a craftsperson who has moulded and engraved the silver into this complicated design. This would add to the cost of the piece.	✓ ✓
I think the teapot would appeal to females more than males as it looks quite dainty. Maybe it would have been used by wealthy ladies for afternoon tea at the time it was made. I imagine it appealing to more mature ladies who like quirky designs. It would be a good 'conversation piece'. Perhaps it was bought as a reminder of Scotland.	✓ ✓
A much more full and detailed response. You have dealt with all aspects of the question very well and opinions are backed up with justification.	10

Architectural/environmental/interior design

In this question, you might be asked about buildings, bridges, shelters, interiors or other man-made structures.

Aberdeen Maritime Museum (1995) designed by Aberdeen City Council

Example H

Architects often have to design new buildings which bridge gaps between existing buildings. Comment on this architectural solution. In your answer, refer to:

- materials
- structure
- colour

How well does this building fit with its surroundings? Give **two** reasons.

Total marks   10

Milwaukee Art Museum (2000) designed by Santiago Calatrava

Example G

Architects consider appearance as well as function when designing new buildings. Comment on this design for an art gallery. In your answer, refer to:

- sources of inspiration
- style
- function

How well has the architect created a building with visual impact? Give **two** reasons.

Total marks   10

Response to example H

Jacob's first attempt – a basic response	Teacher's notes
This building has been constructed using glass and steel girders. There is a lot of glass.	This is a descriptive response. Try to apply what you have learned about architecture in class.
It is a more modern structure than the stone buildings on either side.	What else could you say about its construction? What do you remember about this type of architecture? You could also say how the structure affects the style and function.
A grey blue has been used, maybe to help it blend in with its surroundings.	Try to give more detail here.
This building is different from its surroundings but doesn't look out of place.	You need to give two reasons why this is the case.

Jacob's next attempt	Marks
This building has been constructed using glass and steel girders. This gives a modern, industrial look which is in contrast to the buildings made with more traditional stone on either side. There is a lot of glass used. This means the building is light inside and will make the most of the view.	✓ ✓
The Maritime Museum is a more modern structure than the stone buildings on either side. It has been constructed using the curtain wall technique. This was a method first used by Bauhaus designers and involved the use of steel girders and pillars to create a load-bearing structure. This meant that the wall no longer had to hold the building up, so for the first time large glass windows could be used all around the building. In the interior of the building, the steel girders have been left exposed, maybe as a reminder of the shipbuilding of the past. The girders have round holes cut in them. This would reduce the weight, but also reminds me of port holes, a maritime symbol. Curves are used to soften the straight lines of the girders in the interior and exterior.	✓ ✓ ✓ ✓
The entrance is a revolving door. These are good at allowing the traffic to flow but keep the cold out, which would be important in a cold and windy location .	✓
In the interior, a neutral grey blue has been used, which reflects the colours in the environment. This means that the building blends in well with its surroundings without being too obvious.	✓
This building is very different in style from its surroundings but doesn't look out of place. The large panels of glass reflecting the surroundings also help in this respect. The entrance is small and unobtrusive and there is no obvious signage, which helps the building disappear into its environment.	✓ ✓
A very good response which shows your understanding of architecture.	10

Jewellery design

In jewellery design questions, you may be asked about designs for neckpieces, brooches, bracelets and cuffs, crowns and tiaras, belt buckles, watches and any other body adornments.

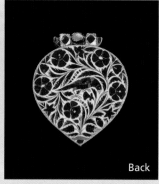

Front

Back

Pendant from India (17th century) by an unknown designer
Gold, diamond, rubies, emeralds, enamel
(Height: 3.7 cm)

Example I

Throughout history, designers have created jewellery. Comment on this pendant design. In your answer, refer to:

- sources of inspiration
- style
- materials

Who might have worn this piece of jewellery? Give **two** reasons.

Total marks   10

Brooch (1901) designed by Georges Fouquet
Gold and enamel
(13 cm × 6.1 cm)

Example J

Jewellery designers often produce pieces with a distinctive style. Comment on this brooch design. In your answer, refer to:

- sources of inspiration
- materials
- target market

What is your opinion on the style of this piece? Give **two** reasons.

Total marks   10

Inflection V/1 neckpiece (1988) designed by David Watkins
Gilded brass, blue and red Colorcore
(Diameter: 31.4 cm)

Example K

Jewellery designers find inspiration in different things. Comment on this design for a neckpiece. In your answer, refer to:

- sources of inspiration
- style
- practicality

What target market might this piece be aimed at? Give **two** reasons.

Total marks   10

Response to example K

Robyn's response	Marks
<u>Sources of Inspiration</u> I would guess that the source of inspiration for this neckpiece was something man-made and mechanical. The shapes and forms remind me of clockwork machinery or cogs and wheels.	✓ ✓
<u>Style</u> The style is modern. It is a bold piece of jewellery because of the large scale. It definitely has visual impact. The main element used is shape. The shapes are regular and geometric. The repeating shapes create a bold pattern. The piece appears to be constructed of two flat pieces, one made of brass and the other of a coloured material. The flat blue of the section underneath contrasts with the warm tones of the brass section on top. These are unconventional materials for jewellery and give an unusual appearance to the neckpiece.	✓ ✓ ✓ ✓
<u>Practicality</u> The neckpiece is not ergonomic; it has not been designed to fit the body. In many ways, it looks quite uncomfortable. The circular form just sits around the neck and might be quite heavy. The protruding parts may be a bit of a health and safety hazard. It is not the most practical piece of jewellery, but I don't think this was the designer's main consideration. I think it is a piece which puts style before practicality, like many fashion and jewellery pieces.	✓ ✓ ✓ ✓
<u>Target Market</u> I think the target market for this neckpiece would be a female collector of unusual designer jewellery. The piece certainly makes a statement and could work well with a plain black dress. I imagine it would only be worn for special occasions because of the lack of practicality. It would have to be worn by a very confident individual as it would get the wearer noticed.	✓ ✓
This was quite a challenging piece to discuss but you have done well. Your exam technique is very good as you have brought in related issues, such as discussing the materials in relation to the style.	10

COMMON MISTAKES

Many candidates run out of things to say when they answer the question in a very restricted way. You often need to expand your response to include related issues. As long as you always make a connection with the main issue being asked about, this is fine and you will gain marks.

HINTS & TIPS

Remember that when you are asked about style, you can discuss how colour, shape, form, pattern and texture have been used.

Fashion/textile design

In this question, you may be asked about designs for any fashion or textile item. Possibilities include historical fashion, catwalk creations, clothing for men, women and children, street style, costumes for theatre and film, uniforms, protective clothing. You could also be asked about textile designs for clothing and interiors.

Costume from the OVO show,
Cirque du Soleil (2009) by Liz Vandal
Printed fabric

Example L

Costume designers have to design outfits that function well and have visual impact. Comment on this design for a character in a circus. In your answer, refer to:

■ function
■ form
■ materials

How effective is the visual impact of this design? Give **two** reasons.

Total marks 10

Ensemble (1879–81) by Halling,
Pearce and Stone
Satin, trimmed with figured silk,
chenille tassels and machine-made
lace, lined with silk and cotton

Example M

Throughout history, fashion designers have experimented with the female silhouette. Comment on this dress design. In your answer, refer to:

■ form
■ wearability
■ materials

Who might have worn this dress?
Give **two** reasons.

Total marks 10

Firefighter's uniform (2012)
Fire-resistant materials
including aramid (Nomex),
PTEF-coated kevlar, kevlar
felt and reflective tape

Example N

Clothing designers often have to consider function as well as appearance. Comment on the design of this uniform. In your answer, refer to:

■ function
■ materials
■ style

How effective is this design? Give **two** reasons.

Total marks 10

Response to example N

Amy's first descriptive response	Amy's second more analytical response
Function	Function
The function is a uniform for a firefighter. It has gloves, a helmet and a mask.	The function is a uniform for a firefighter. It has a protective function, so will need to be tough and durable and be able to withstand extreme conditions. There are protective gloves, boots and headwear. The helmet will protect the firefighter from falling objects. A mask is also included in case the firefighter needs to breathe in smoky conditions. It will also protect their face and eyes from debris. As it is a uniform it also has an identity function. It is important that firefighters can recognise each other and that members of the public can tell who the firefighters are.
Materials	Materials
The materials used are fire resistant. The uniform is a dull yellow with brighter yellow stripes.	The materials used are fire resistant. This is important given the job that firefighters do. They may need to enter burning buildings and so their clothing must not be flammable. The uniform is a dull yellow with brighter yellow stripes made of reflective tape. This is so that firefighters can be seen in low visibility conditions. The gloves and knees of the uniform look as if they are padded. This will be to protect their hands from heat and their knees if they have to crawl through small spaces or get down onto the ground.
Style	Style
The style is baggy with lots of pockets.	Practicality is more important than style, but the distinctive yellow colour, high visibility stripes and helmet make it instantly recognisable as a firefighter's uniform. The shape is baggy, presumably to make it easy to move in. There are lots of pockets to allow firefighters to carry all their equipment.
Effectiveness	Effectiveness
I think this design will be effective. **These are valid observations and opinions. Now try to develop these by thinking about reasons why.**	I think this design will be effective, as uniforms like this have been used for some time now and have not been replaced with anything better. The main purpose is to protect the firefighter and it seems well designed to do this as the person's body is completely covered. **Much fuller and more detailed responses. Good work!**

Chapter 5

Critical Studies Wordbanks

To complete your Critical Studies successfully and do well in the Question Paper, it is important to extend your range of vocabulary and build up a good understanding of Art & Design terminology.

We will start with the **visual elements**, which artists and designers use in different combinations for visual effect.

The visual elements

Line

Line can be used to show shape and form when drawing or painting.

Texture and pattern can be represented through line.

Line can express mood and emotion in expressive art.

In design, line can be used to communicate ideas and can affect the style of a design.

Words about line					
thick	angular	outline	flowing	zigzag	continuous
thin	rectilinear	horizontal	graceful	jagged	broken
broad	rough	vertical	elegant	twisting	ragged
straight	textural	diagonal	precise	cross-hatched	scratchy
curved	expressive	wavy	accurate	stripe	inconsistent
long	bold	curvilinear	sensitive	neat	freehand
short	confident	fluid	delicate	sketchy	gestural
hard	hesitant	smooth	controlled	faint	spontaneous
light	fine	squiggly	definite	subtle	

Tone

Tone can be used to show the variation from light to dark.

Tone can be used in drawing to describe 3D form, pattern and texture.

The direction and source of light in a drawing or painting can be shown through tone.

Tone can be used expressively or to create a sense of realism or to show mood and atmosphere.

Words about tone					
light	highlight	limited tonal range	dramatic	hard light	drab
dark	half-tone	wide tonal range	contrasting	diffused light	faded
soft	mid-tone	tonal value	exaggerated	high key	sombre
subtle	monotone	tonal scale	hard	low key	gloomy
muted	graduated	light source	glowing	reflected light	murky
gradation	graded	direction of light	luminous	reflection	dim
blended	shaded	shadow	illuminated	bright	flat

Colour

Colour can convey mood in expressive art.

We often associate colour with emotion.

Colour can be used to enhance a design or to attract a certain target market.

In design, colour can contribute to style.

Words about colour			
primary	transparent	bright	monochromatic
secondary	opaque	strong	neutral
tertiary	hue	harsh	subtle
complementary	pigment	vibrant	restrained
opposite	tone	intense	limited palette
contrasting	tint	saturated	restricted palette
harmonious	balanced	bold	pale
related	varied	deep	muted
hot/warm	deep	vivid	faded
cold/cool	fluorescent	rich	realistic
symbolic	luminescent	expressive	naturalistic
decorative	pearlescent	exaggerated	life-like
advancing	iridescent	clashing	earthy
receding	lurid	gaudy	delicate
balanced	loud	garish	weak
blended	brilliant	polychromatic	washed out
reflected colour	kaleidoscopic	multi-coloured	pure

The colour wheel

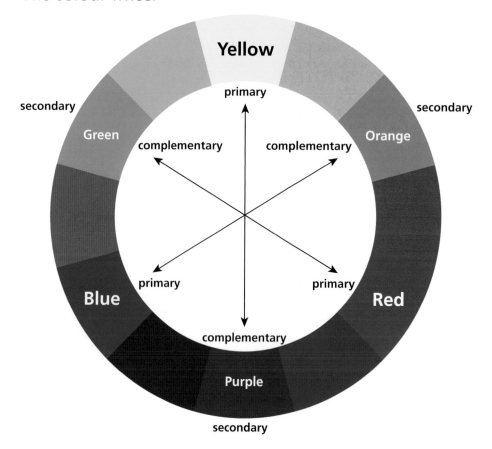

Primary colours

Primary colours cannot be mixed using other colours. Red, yellow and blue are primary colours.

Harmonious colours

These are the groups of colours that are next to each other on the colour wheel – for example, green, turquoise and blue, or red, orange and yellow. They are sometimes called analogous colours.

Complementary colours

Complementary colours are opposite each other on the colour wheel. For this reason, they are sometimes called opposite colours. When used together, they tend to clash.

Secondary colours

Secondary colours are made by mixing two primary colours. These are purple (blue and red), orange (red and yellow) and green (blue and yellow).

Tertiary colours

Tertiary colours are made by mixing the three primary colours together. Depending on the amount of each colour, different results will be achieved. Tertiary colours are a variety of browns or greys.

Tints, tones and shades

Tints are made by adding a colour to white.

Tones are made by adding grey to a colour.

Shades are made by adding black to a colour.

Texture

Texture can be used to describe how a surface feels or looks.

Texture can be represented using 2D techniques.

3D techniques can be used to create surface texture.

Words about texture			
tactile	furry	even	brushstroke
touch	scaly	uneven	impasto
textural	silky	grainy	bas relief
soft	hairy	indented	low relief
hard	rippled	pitted	linear
rough	wrinkled	dusty	swirling
smooth	crinkled	waxy	dashed
coarse	ribbed	greasy	directional
fine	grooved	velvety	random
flat	spiky	fleecy	bumpy
shiny	scratched	woolly	woven
glossy	abrasive	matt	

Shape

Shape defines a two-dimensional area.

Shape can help to communicate design ideas and can contribute to the style of a design.

Shapes can be repeated to make patterns.

Form

Form is three-dimensional shape.

Form can be used in sculpture, low relief work or in 3D design.

In expressive art, form can be used to show realism.

In design, form can contribute to style.

| sphere | cube | cylinder | cone | pyramid |

Words about shape and form

Shape and form		Shape	Form	
regular	simple	circular	sphere	sculptural
irregular	complex	rectangular	cube	architectural
geometric	fragmented	oblong	cylinder	profile
organic	jagged	square	pyramid	relief
man-made	pointed	triangular	cone	moulded
natural	distorted	oval	conical	sculpted
angular	freeform	pentagon	helix	modelled
rounded	bold	hexagon	spherical	carved
symmetrical	distinct	octagon	cuboid	built
asymmetrical	indistinct	outlined	triangular	constructed
flat	spiral	positive	tactile	assembled
repeating	twisted	negative	textural	tool marks
elongated	large-scale	overlapping	massive	solid
simplified	small-scale	silhouette	monumental	hard
stylised	short	negative space	hollow	
spiky	tall	amorphous	light	
hard-edged	wide	nebulous	heavy	
soft	narrow	fluid	mass	

Pattern

Pattern is an arrangement of repeating elements or motifs: lines; shapes; forms; tones; or colours.

Pattern can be used to enhance expressive artwork or design ideas.

Pattern can be found in the natural and man-made environments.

Words about pattern			
applied	random	dots	decorative
repeating	varied	polka dot	ornate
simple	regular	dashes	ornamental
complex	linear	lines	embellished
man-made	rectilinear	stripes	bold
natural	curvilinear	chequered	subtle
geometric	rhythmic	tartan	clashing
organic	symmetrical	plaid	kinetic
mechanical	asymmetrical	floral	optical
motifs	symbols	speckled	digital
squiggles	mirror image	marbled	abstract
large-scale	multi-directional	cross-hatched	psychedelic
small-scale	half-drop	stippled	tessellated

Expressive art

Composition

Composition is the arrangement of elements within a painting, drawing or photograph.

In sculpture, composition is about the spatial arrangement of 3D forms.

Artists use composition to lead the viewer's eye around the work in a particular way.

Words about composition				
arrangement	viewpoint	focal point	subject	sitter (in portraiture)
foreground	framed	centre of interest	object	subject matter
middleground	cropped	point(s) of interest	distorted	frame within frame
background	close-up	elevated viewpoint	fragmented	in proportion
horizontal	wide angle	camera angle	symmetrical	out of proportion
vertical	circular	eye-level	asymmetrical	portrait orientation
diagonal	triangular	bird's eye view	balanced	landscape orientation
linear	staged	low viewpoint	busy	one-point perspective
horizon line	set up	picture plane	cluttered	two-point perspective
perspective	dynamic	negative space	crowded	flattened perspective
leading line	small-scale	rule of thirds	minimalist	aerial perspective
s-curve	large-scale	depth of field	sparse	vanishing point

Mood and atmosphere

By using different combinations of the visual elements and a variety of techniques, artists can create a variety of different moods in their work.

Words about mood and atmosphere				
tranquil	exciting	atmospheric	violent	sad
peaceful	busy	overcast	disordered	pessimistic
quiet	fun	gloomy	aggressive	melancholy
serene	happy	sunlit	hostile	depressing
calm	joyful	sun-drenched	moody	dismal
informal	passionate	shadowy	intense	desolate
relaxed	flamboyant	warm	threatening	lonely
still	lively	cold	disturbing	sensitive
undisturbed	optimistic	leaden	powerful	thought provoking
controlled	emotional	dreary	inspiring	moving
dispassionate	expressive	lack-lustre	poignant	breathtaking

Design

Aesthetics and style

Aesthetics is about appearance.

Each designer has their own distinctive style which affects the appearance of their designs.

Different aesthetics appeal to different target audiences.

The visual elements will affect the style of a design, so you should refer to these wordbanks as well.

Words about aesthetics and style			
line	antique	gothic	appealing
colour	traditional	rococo	attractive
shape	classical	baroque	visual impact
form	Victoriana	romantic	decorative
pattern	minimalist	Arts and Crafts	ornamental
texture	vintage	Art Nouveau	sophisticated
source of inspiration	retro	Art Deco	elegant
influences	futuristic	modernist	sculptural
the 'look'	industrial	punk	tasteful
appearance	original	contemporary	flashy
layout	quirky	up-to-date	experimental
arrangement	idiosyncratic	sleek	eclectic
text	kitsch	streamlined	eccentric
font	avant-garde	fun	statement piece
use of space	ahead of its time	funky	conversation piece

Function

Function is about the purpose of a design.

Designers have to consider functional issues, even in very decorative pieces.

Words about function			
purpose	ergonomics	durability	eco-friendly
intention	user-friendly	fragile	sustainability
rationale	technological	delicate	safety
protoype	mechanical	built in obsolescence	risk
concept	high-tech	disposable	danger
fitness for purpose	digital	hard-wearing	hazard
functionality	computerised	robust	secure
wearability (fashion)	microtechnology	sturdy	protection
suitability	nanotechnology	built to last	weight
practicality	robotic	multi-functional	scale

Target market

Designers have to consider their target market, whether this is one client,
a specific group or the mass market.

Words about target market			
design brief	gender	age group	cost
client	male	age bracket	budget
specification	female	babies	added value
commission	unisex	children	income bracket
one-off	designer label	teenagers	disposable income
limited edition	diffusion line	young adults	customer type
mass produced	high street	adults	socioeconomic group
mass-market	middle-market	couples	cost effective
disposable	commercial	families	status symbol
sustainable	trendy	general public	value for money
eco-friendly	fashionable	demographic	promotion
market research	exclusive	niche market	persuasion
market forces	target audience	up-market	consumer appeal

Chapter 6

External Assessment: Portfolio Gallery

Candidate A

Your National 5 Expressive and Design Portfolios are submitted to SQA to be marked. Your work is suspended from racks while it is being marked. The work from your school is hung up in alphabetical order.

HINTS & TIPS

You are allowed to submit **up to** the equivalent of 3 × A2 sheets for each Portfolio. This can be presented in a variety of formats, as appropriate (for example, 4 × A3 plus 1 × A2).

Candidate B

Some possible Portfolio formats

Area per folio

3D Model

Chapter 7

Useful Resources

National Gallery	www.nationalgallery.org.uk
National Portrait Gallery	www.npg.org.uk
Tate Galleries	www.tate.org.uk
British Museum	www.britishmuseum.org
Crafts Council	www.craftscouncil.org.uk
Design Museum	www.designmuseum.org
Victoria & Albert Museum	www.vam.ac.uk
Design Council	www.designcouncil.org.uk
National Gallery, Scotland	www.nationalgalleries.org
Pompidou Centre, Paris	www.centrepompidou.fr
Guggenheim Museum	www.guggenheim.org
Museum of Modern Art, New York	www.moma.org
Courtauld Gallery	www.courtauld.ac.uk/gallery
Institute of Contemporary Art	www.ica.org.uk
Saatchi Gallery	www.saatchi-gallery.org.uk
White Cube	www.whitecube.com
Flowers Gallery	www.flowersgallery.com
Imperial War Museum	www.iwm.org.uk
British Journal of Photograph	www.bjphoto.co.uk
National Media Museum	www.nationalmediamuseum.org.uk
Magnum Photos	www.magnumphotos.com
Artist Encyclopaedia	www.artcyclopedia.com
Web Museum online art gallery	www.ibiblio.org/wm
Museum and gallery websites collection	www.gallerywebsites.co.uk
Image website	www.pinterest.com
Historical Fashion & Costume	www.costumegallery.com
How to hand embroider	www.inaminuteago.com
International Feltmakers Association	www.feltmakers.com
Textile artists' group	www.62group.org.uk
Public Monuments and Sculpture Association	www.pmsa.org.uk
Dazzle jewellery	www.dazzle-exhibitions.com
Contemporary jewellery	www.velvetdavinci.com
Contemporary jewellery	www.klimt02.net
Graphics – Packaging design	www.lovelypackage.com/
Fashion	www.style.com
British Vogue magazine	www.vogue.co.uk
Royal Institute of British Architects	www.architecture.com
Architectural Association	www.aaschool.ac.uk

Acknowledgements

We would like to thank a number of people who made this book possible:

The Art & Design pupils of James Hamilton Academy, Mearns Castle High School and Kilmarnock Academy, with particular thanks to Sanna Ahmad, Robyn Anderson, Eamon Grady, Amy Murray, Emily Raine, Beth Wilson and Darren Wylie for the examples of artwork, Nicolle Phillips for the cover photograph, and to Anna Cunningham, Aimee McCabe and David Cameron for contributing photographs.

Our head teachers, Janis Teale and Dean Smith, who continue to value and support Art & Design education.

John Mitchell and Elizabeth Fletcher at Hodder Gibson for having faith in our original vision.

Our colleagues at school and SQA for being passionate about Art & Design and for contributing to the development of the approaches in this book, with special mention to Asmara Azeem, Tia Campbell, Gaynor Catterson, Zandra Gatti, Andy Latto, Hugh Mackay, Kirsty McKee, Susan Miller, David Marshall and Caroline Stewart.

Last, but certainly not least, thanks to John Kirkland, Andy and Josh Lightbown (and Diesel the dog!) for putting up with being neglected during the writing of this book.